THE KEY TO ART

THE KEY TO GOTHIC ART

José Bracons
Professor of Art History

Lerner Publications Company • Minneapolis

Words that appear in **bold** type are listed in the glossary.

This edition published 1990
by Lerner Publications Company
241 First Avenue North, Minneapolis, Minnesota 55401, USA

In association with David Bateman Ltd.
32-34 View Road, Glenfield, Auckland, New Zealand

LIBRARY OF CONGRESS CATALOGING-IN-PUBLICATION DATA

Bracons i Clapés, Josep.
[Claves del arte gótico. English]
The key to gothic art / Jose Bracons.
p. cm.–(The Key to art)
Translation of: Las claves del arte gótico.
Includes index.
Summary: Discusses the history and characteristics of Gothic art, as represented in architecture, illuminated manuscripts, painting, stained glass, and sculpture.
ISBN 0-8225-2051-6 (lib. bdg.)
ISBN 0-8225-2054-0 (pbk.)
1. Art, Gothic–Themes, motives. 2. Art appreciation. [1. Art, Gothic.] I. Title. II. Series.
N6310.B7313 1990
709.02′2–dc20 89-12223
CIP
AC

A David Bateman Book

Printed in Spain
Bound in USA by Muscle Bound Bindery

1 2 3 4 5 6 7 8 9 10 99 98 97 96 95 94 93 92 91 90

INTRODUCTION

'he Royal Doors. :hartres Cathedral. 145-55. Chartres, rance.
'his entrance at the :hartres Cathedral in rance is the first major xample of a Gothic oorway. In contrast to oors built in the Roman- sque style, the tympanums the triangular areas nder the arches—are omplemented by sculp- ire. The center tympanum epresents the majesty of od. The scenes to either de represent the Virgin lary and the Ascension of hrist. Kings, queens, and atriarchs from the Old estament appear on the ipporting pillars. The ifferent styles show that everal artists or groups of tists must have worked n the doors.

The Appreciation of Gothic Art

The term *Gothic art* refers to European art and architecture from the middle of the 12th century to the early 16th century. The art of this period was scorned by the leaders of the Italian Renaissance—the cultural movement that followed the Gothic period. Giorgio Vasari described the art forms of earlier periods as "a reflection of the art invented by the Goths who, having destroyed ancient buildings and slaughtered their architects in battle, covered vaults with pointed arches and covered Italy with a rash of accursed buildings of a type that we hope will never again be built."

Vasari and other Renaissance thinkers saw a clear distinction between Gothic art and architecture and Roman art and architecture. They believed that Roman art embodied the classical

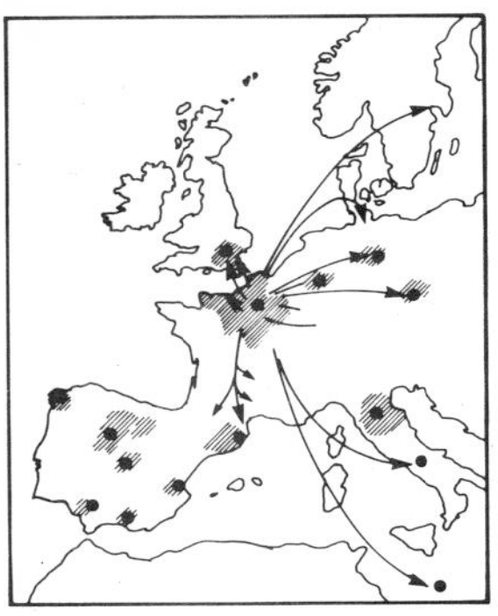

GOTHIC EUROPE
The Gothic style began in France. It spread across Europe and was accepted and adapted in various ways in different countries. Later Gothic art was redefined in Italy, in a way that influenced art in the rest of Europe. The final period of Gothic art, which coincided with the blossoming of the Renaissance movement in Italy, took place mainly in Burgundy, Flanders, and Germany.

Renaissance ideal that was closer to perfectio Vasari ends his comments by praying that "Gc will now free all countries from all forms thinking and building that clash with the beau of ours."

This idea that the classical style was best laste for several centuries and resulted in scornful r jection of all that was medieval. It was not un the Romantic movement in art began in the 18 century that the Gothic tradition was revive From then on, Romantic artists got their inspir tion from medieval art and architecture. The ter *Gothic* gradually overcame its negative meaning

Gothic art existed over a period of four ce turies. It has no common denominator. We mu try to understand the extraordinary geograph diversity of Gothic art and the many politic religious, and economic pressures that affect the Gothic style.

Geographical and Chronological Expansion of Gothic Art

The Gothic period lasted from the midd of the 12th century until the first decad of the 16th century. Within this time spa Gothic art was found from Spain to Scandinav and from Ireland to the eastern borders of tl Holy Roman Empire. The military, commerci and religious activities of western Europea in the eastern Mediterranean area explains wl Gothic art was also found on the islands Rhodes and Cyprus and in other spots in tl Middle East.

The Gothic style continued to be popular i many countries, even after the 16th century. England, for example, the Gothic tradition serve as inspiration for artists of the Neo-Gothic reviv of the 19th century.

Western facade. Cathedral of Notre Dame. c. 1210. Paris, France. This facade, or building front, is a good example of the first phase of Gothic art. It is noteworthy for the balance between the individual parts of the building. The three main vertical elements are built on three massive doors. The sides are crowned by high towers. The cathedral also has a three-level division: the doors, the royal gallery, and upper gallery and towers.

REGINALD ELY and others. King's College Chapel. c. 1466. Cambridge, England. Perpendicular Gothic architecture appeared in England in the middle of the 14th century. As the name implies, perpendicular lines make up the decorative elements of this style. Fan vaulting—a design unique to England—and tall, slim windows are also important elements. King's College Chapel is an excellent example of the English Perpendicular style. The structure of the building itself is very simple. It consists of a lofty central hall flooded with light. The chapel was not completed until the 16th century.

There was a basic difference in the development of Gothic architecture in northern and southern Europe. At times, the two styles contradicted each other, yet they also complemented one another.

The development of Gothic art is usually divided into three main phases: an initial period during which Gothic form was first defined; a middle period during which the classic Gothic style developed and expanded; and a final period dominated by the tastes of the aristocracy and middle class.

Within these general phases, there are a large number of subdivisions. In France, there was an initial Gothic architectural style, followed by Classic, Rayonnant, and Flamboyant styles. In England, we find Early English, Decorated, and Perpendicular architecture styles.

In the field of painting, a linear style evolved as well as a style known as 1200 or Byzantine

There was a period of Italian domination in painting, followed by an international period, followed by a period when painting was mainly influenced by Flemish and Burgundian artists. There are no such clearly defined subdivisions in sculpture during the Gothic period.

Historic Milestones of Gothic Art

To understand Gothic art, we must keep in mind the historical, cultural, and social factors that shaped it. The 12th century was the century of European expansion. A population explosion and improved methods of agriculture and trade improved the economy of the area. Pilgrimages and crusades expanded European and Christian influence during this time. In Spain, the Spanish Christians overthrew the Moors, and the Germanic world started its advance toward the East.

The 12th century also saw great monastic reforms. New towns and cities developed and became centers of culture and scholarship. Cathedral schools in towns replaced monasteries as centers of learning.

During the 12th century the feudal system was replaced by a growing acceptance of the power of the king. France, where this process was strongest, was the cradle of Gothic art. By the 13th century, the institution of monarchy was firmly established. This was the century of Louis IX—Saint Louis—of France, Edward I of England, Frederick II of Germany, and Alfonso the Wise of Spain. With the restoration of the power of the monarchs, distinct nations began to emerge. Great cultural activity developed, started mainly by the monarchs themselves. All this strengthened feelings of national pride.

***The Canticles of Saint Mary*. Frontispiece. pre-1284. Library of the Escorial Monastery, El Escorial, Spain.**
The Canticles of Saint Mary were written by Alfonso X (called "The Wise") of Castile in Spain. Alfonso ordered the miniaturists of his court to illustrate the canticles or songs. The texts praise the Virgin Mary and tell of miraculous deeds that she brought about. The texts were written to be set to music. This explains the musical notations on the manuscript. The illustrations give a fresh vision of daily life and spirituality during the 13th century. In the page reproduced here, the wise king sits in his palace. He dictates words and music as singers and musicians prepare to perform.

GIOTTO.
***Saint Francis Preaching to the Birds.* pre-1307.**
The Basilica, Assisi, Italy.
The Franciscan order deeply influenced the art of the Gothic period, particularly in Italy. The Basilica at Assisi was the starting point for many innovations in painting and architecture. The interior decoration, thought to be the work of Giotto, depicts various events, including Saint Francis preaching to the birds. This scene clearly shows the Franciscan idea that every creature is a sign of God. With very little detail, Giotto suggests a natural environment. While many people are certain that these paintings were done by Giotto and collaborators, some art historians tend to doubt this.

The 13th century was also a time of economic prosperity. The textile industry grew in Europe. New urban centers, and the roads linking them, were the scenes of extraordinary activity and commerce. The growth of the cities triggered development in new social organizations. Craftspeople and merchants organized guilds—groups of people with the same professions or skills. A new middle-class population took control of city government.

The spiritual life of the 13th century was shaped in large part by the development of the towns and the appearance of new religious orders such as the Franciscans and the Dominicans. The new religious orders influenced both the common

eople and the world of culture and art.

Universities became important centers of learn-ıg during the 13th century. Two great lines of ıought spread through the universities—that of aint Francis and that of Saint Thomas Aquinas. .quinas's *Treatises* sum up the intellectual activ-y of the age.

The 13th century is considered to have been ıe greatest period of medieval splendor. At the nd of that century, economic expansion reached s peak.

European society entered a time of crisis during ıe 14th century. The settlement and develop-ıent of new land, which was becoming scarcer, egan to lag. Agricultural production declined ıbstantially. This caused grave fear among rural eople.

Trade also suffered, and the economy slumped. he effects of hunger and inflation were felt most ı the cities and among the poorer classes. Great

AMBROGIO LORENZETTI. ***Good Government of the City*. 1338-39. Palazzo Pubblico, Siena, Italy.**

In the decoration of one of the chambers in the city hall, the city council of Siena, Italy, chose to show the ways of good government and tyranny side by side. Clearly, behind this decision lay the wish to make a statement about good government during a time of political uncertainty. The effects of good government are shown in the happiness of the citizens, the prosperity of the craftspeople, and the elegance of the nobility.

Papal Palace. 14th century. Avignon, France. Because of power clashes between the church and the state, the French pope, Clement V, moved the seat of the papacy to Avignon in France. The popes resided there between 1309 and 1367 and built for themselves an impressive fortified palace overlooking the city and close to the cathedral. A number of buildings were erected. Pierre Poisson and Jean de Louvres, two of the architects who worked with Italian artists on the project, made Avignon a center of southern Gothic art.

epidemics spread, the worst being the Black Death, or plague, of 1348 and 1349.

The greatest political crisis of the 14th century was the Hundred Years War between France and England. During this same century, conflicts within the Roman Catholic church and clashes between church and state added to Europe's distress. The temporary transfer of the papacy to Avignon, France, and the Great Schism, in which several churchmen claimed to be the rightful pope, caused political and spiritual distress. In response, many new religious movements sprang up.

Another reaction to the crisis was a concentration of political power into the hands of a few rulers. The pope, too, acquired greater authority over the everyday lives of the people.

At the same time, there was a historical phenomenon with an enormous potential to change medieval life and culture. This was the development of capitalism, an economic system based on private ownership and free enterprise. This system fostered new ideas, such as a vision of the world based on critical thought and individual accomplishments. People recovered their strength and optimism by going against the

ENGUERRAND QUARTON. ***Pietà of Villeneuve-les-Avignon.*** **1455. The Louvre, Paris, France.** Gothic painting sought a closer representation of reality, although it can scarcely be described as realistic. At first, the donors who had commissioned the works were shown in the paintings with Mary and the saints. Then the donors gradually became the principal figures in paintings. The donor in this painting is magnificently depicted along with Saint John, who was probably his patron saint. The intense drama of the scene is concentrated upon the body of Christ. The golden background, showing just the silhouette of a city, gives the picture a timeless dimension.

established values of the church. They produced a non-religious culture and made advances in scientific discovery. The new values were translated into art forms during the first waves of the Renaissance.

Art and Society During the Gothic Period

During the early Gothic period, the artist was not considered as important as the craftsperson. Medieval society valued technical skills more than creative ability. The artist was not expected to develop artistic theories or new methods of painting. In most cases, the artist was only expected to reproduce standard figures and images and carry out the instructions of people who were considered to be on a "higher" cultural level.

Gradually, the role of the artist grew. Artists began to sign their works in order to be credited with them. Mateo carved his name on the lintel of the Portico de la Gloria in 1188. Giovanni Pisano did the same on the pulpit of the baptistery at the cathedral at Siena. Jan van Eyck left proof of his presence at the marriage of Giovanni Arnolfini by signing his wedding portrait, "Jan van Eyck was here." In general, architectural work

VILLARD DE HONNECOURT. Interior and exterior of a chapel in Reims Cathedral. Early 13th century. National Library, Paris, France.
Villard de Honnecourt was an architect from Picardy in France. Though we cannot identify for certain any buildings Villard designed, his drawings and his notes are necessary for

and sculptures were more frequently signed thar were paintings and small objects.

Like other craft groups during the Middle Ages artists began to organize themselves into guilds and brotherhoods. Only a few artists were successful at more than one specialty. Among those engaged in building, a clear distinction was made between the master of the project—the architect or the engineer—and the simple bricklayer, mason (stoneworker), or craftsperson Builders' associations—called lodges—were closed and secretive societies. The guilds and lodges were involved with all the great building projects of the age. Guild members made sure that their technical skills would be passed on to the nex generation by training young apprentices.

The studios and workshops of painters sculptors, goldsmiths, and silversmiths fulfilled a similar function. It was rare for a craftsperson of any importance not to have at his side an apprentice, a collaborator, a servant, or a relative to whom he imparted the skills of his profession It is usually assumed that the master was responsible for the design of a work and for its final phases. The assistants did the preparatory work. Based on this assumption, art historian distinguish the works of the medieval maste from those of the apprentices by the quality o the finished work.

As cities expanded during the Gothic period artists and craftspeople gathered in urban center where there was a growing market for their skills However, most artists of the 13th, 14th, and 15t centuries did not remain in one location. Painter and precious metal workers did carry on thei professions from studios and workshops. Bu architects, sculptors, and fresco painters had t be constantly on the move. During this period

our understanding of Gothic architecture. He visited various countries and drew many buildings, but concentrated on the cathedral at Reims, noting many of its details. The drawings reproduced here show one of the cathedral's chapels. That chapel looks basically the same today.

GIOVANNI PISANO. *Virgin and Child.* c. 1305. Arena Chapel, Padua, Italy.
This Virgin and Child is developed upon similar images found in many French cathedrals and with which the artist would have been familiar. French paintings of the Virgin, however, tend to emphasize the grace of the mother-son relationship. Here, the artist chose to portray the tension of the relationship. Note the artist's signature along the base of the statue.

ANONYMOUS.
The Wilton Diptych.
c. 1400. National Gallery, London, England.
The theme of this work is the presentation of King Richard II to the Virgin Mary by John the Baptist, Edward the Confessor, and Saint Edmund. King Richard is depicted as a beardless youngster, although we know that the work was begun during the last years of his life. Perhaps it was not finished until after Richard's death. The king's features have been painted to be in harmony with those of the heavenly court preparing to receive him. The variation in shade

artists began to specialize and to develop individual styles.

As society became more complex during the Middle Ages, more written documents were created about the lives of artists and about their artistic creations. It thus becomes easier to link works with the artists who created them and to compile biographies of certain artists. Learning how artists lived and worked gives us a better understanding of each artist's creations. The amount of written material about the lives of artists that survives from the Middle Ages varies greatly from country to country.

Most artists worked on the basis of individual commissions. That is, the artist would agree to create a work for a client for a fee. Contracts between artists and clients are a source of very important information for art historians. They specify not only the artistic taste of the client, but so prices, delivery dates, where the work was to e carried out, quality of materials, and the rocedures to be followed.

Commissions from royalty and the upper class tracted the highest quality of workmanship. he desire for self-promotion and a spirit of xury and display were always present in the eat courts of Europe. But we must also take into count the influence of the middle class. Though e origins of Gothic art are tightly bound up ith the ruling class, there came a time when the iddle class assumed the major role in influencg the Gothic style. The middle class insisted n a new sense of realism. This influence can be en in the architecture of the time in craft halls, wn halls, marketplaces, government buildings, d palaces.

Many of the great works of a religious nature hurches, chapels, altarpieces, tombs, ornaents, and books) were commissioned by either yal or middle-class patrons.

Just as we can distinguish differences among orks by different types of patrons, we can also e that among artists themselves, there were uite noticeable social differences. Giotto was ry well paid for his work. He owned and rented t land and loaned out large sums of money. Jan n Eyck was a close friend of the Duke of urgundy and undertook several political issions on the duke's behalf. These two are ceptional cases, but they demonstrate the high cial levels that could be attained by an artist uring the Gothic period.

There was little distinction made between rge and small works of art during the Middle ges. In fact, less importance was often attached large, monumental works than to small aintings, jewelry, and precious metalwork.

and tone of the celestial blue clothing is truly impressive. The elegance and refinement of the work is typical of the international Gothic style.

The Door of Judgment. Early 13th century. Notre Dame Cathedral, Paris, France.
The Last Judgment is a theme often used on Gothic doors. Here, Christ appears with the wounds of the Crucifixion, according to the description in Saint Matthew's Gospel. Angels are grouped around him, as are Saint John and the Virgin Mary. On the lower half of the door, the blessed are shown to be separated from the damned. The Resurrection is depicted on the lintel—the horizontal piece over the center of the door. Angels, saints, and characters from the Old Testament are shown on the arch.

ARCHITECTURE

SIMÓN DE COLOGNE. Constable's Chapel. 1482-94. Burgos Cathedral, Burgos, Spain. This chapel was used by Pedro Fernandez de Velasco and his wife as a funeral chapel. The chapel was designed by Simón de Cologne, who made it strikingly different from the rest of the cathedral at Burgos in Spain. The star-shaped vault, in which some panels have been replaced with stained glass, seems to float above the chapel.

Gothic architecture began in the Île-de-France, a province in northern France, and expanded outward. The main religious center in this area was the Abbey of Saint-Denis. The abbey was the tomb of the saint, burial site of the French kings, and the storage place for the royal emblems and jewels.

In 1122, Suger became the abbot of Saint-Denis. He devoted himself to the restoration of power to the French monarchy. He also began the restoration of the abbey buildings at Saint-Denis. Work started at the west end of the abbey. The main **facade**, or front, of the new abbey was consecrated in 1140. Suger later undertook the renovation of the eastern end of the abbey, including the **ambulatory**—a sheltered area for walking—and the side chapels.

The main architectural elements in these reconstructions were pointed **arches** and **vaults** (arched roofs or ceilings). These elements were taken from Romanesque architecture of earlier centuries. However, they were combined in a fresh way, according to theories offered by Suger in his writings.

It was this new style of architecture developed at Saint-Denis that was to become the starting point for all Gothic architecture.

The design of the Abbey of Saint-Denis was soon adapted and incorporated into all the major building projects undertaken by the monarchy of France. These projects were undertaken with a

Abbey of Saint-Denis. 1140-1281. Saint-Denis, France.
A landmark in French architecture, the Abbey of Saint-Denis was the inspiration of all Gothic cathedral builders. One hundred years after the consecration of the west front and sections of the nave, Pierre de Montreuil began work on the choir and transepts. The transept

constant striving for perfection. Within a brief time span, emerging Gothic architecture reached its peak. It became an artistic style representing the power of the French throne.

It is impossible to give one definition for Gothic architecture in all of Europe, because the style has so many varied elements. But the **cathedral** combines most of the elements that were to become the hallmarks of Gothic architecture. Cathedrals were episcopal seats (headquarters for bishops) and they became the cultural ymbols of 12th-century European cities.

A main element of the Gothic cathedral is the b vault—a vault with crossed, pointed arches. his vault is based on a very old design. It was sed in Romanesque buildings such as Durham athedral in England and the Church of Saint ephen in Caen in France.

The rib vault is a dynamic structure. Its skeleton f ribs carries the weight of the walls from the **eystone** (the wedge-shaped piece at the top of e arches that locks the other pieces in place) utward and downward to chosen areas. The rib ault is easier to build than some other types f vaults. Rib vaults made it possible to cover uge, open spaces in churches such as aisles, **resbyteries**, and side chapels.

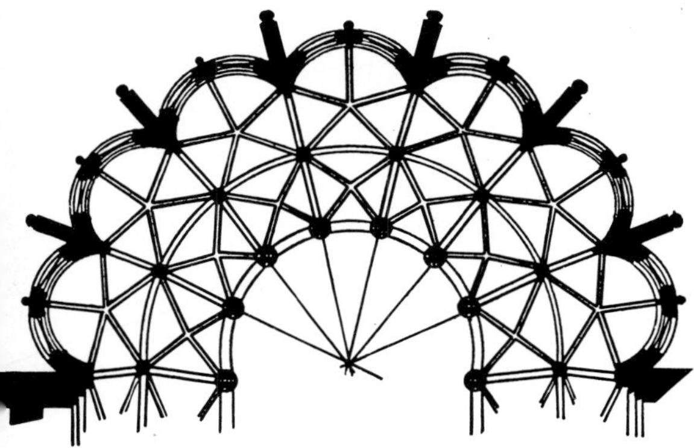

an of the apse and nbulatory at the Abbey Saint-Denis. 1144. int-Denis, France. his writings, Suger compares the building with the mple of Solomon and plains the symbolism of ch element. The columns are said to represent the prophets and the apostles. The keystone is the image of Christ. The light that filters through the stained glass was meant to show humanity the way to the true light of God.

triforium was filled with stained glass. The appearance of the cathedral today owes much to the work of Viollet-le-Duc, who restored it between 1858 and 1879.

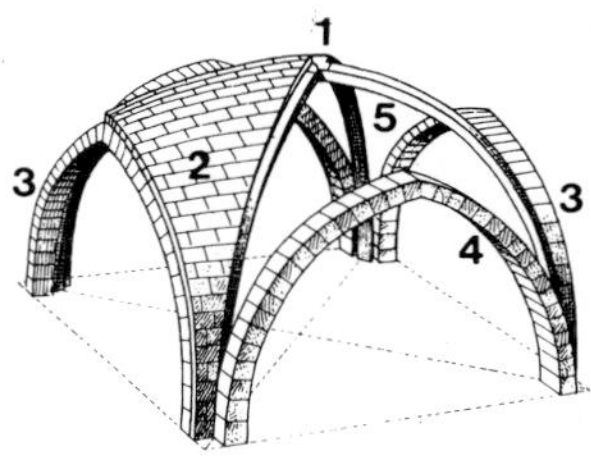

The rib vault
1. Keystone 2. Panel
3. Transverse arches
4. Shaped arches
5. Architectural ribs

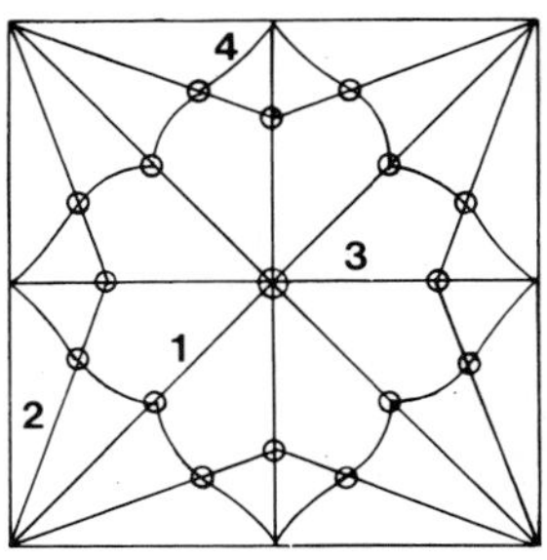

Design of a star-shaped vault
1. Diagonal ribs
2. Secondary ribs 3. Transverse ribs 4. Curved ribs

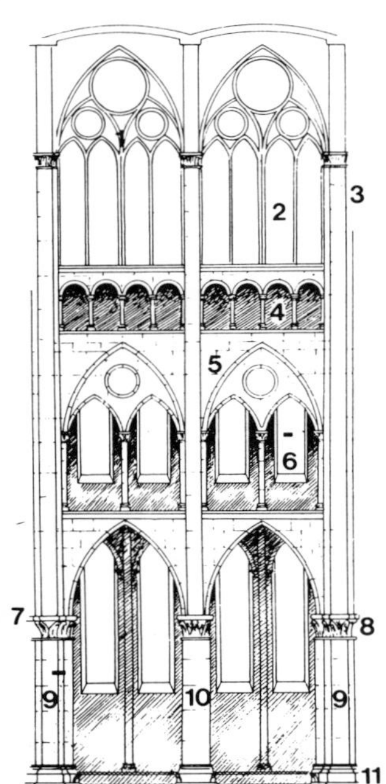

Wall plan of a Gothic cathedral
1. Tracery 2. Lancet windows 3. Clerestory 4. Triforium 5. Supporting arch 6. Gallery 7. Abacus 8. Capital 9. Buttress 10. Cylindrical pillar 11. Base

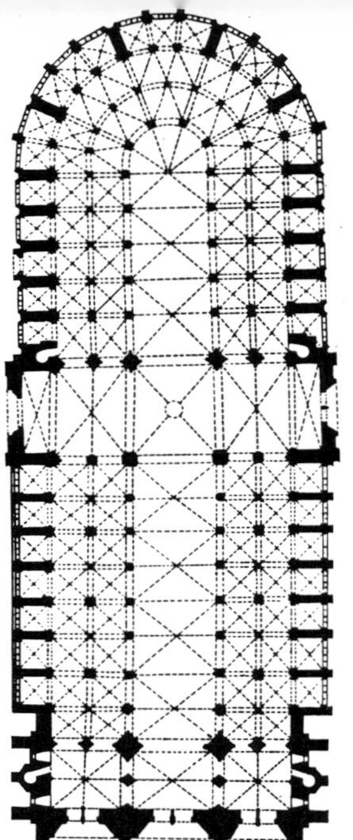

Ground plan of Notre Dame Cathedral. c. 1163 Paris, France.
The Notre Dame Cathedral was far larger than anything built before it. It consisted of a nave with double side aisles. Flying buttresses were fully integrated into the architectural design.

The earliest type of rib vault was compose of two interlinked, pointed arches. These arche divided the vault into four segments. This i known as a quadripartite (or four-parted) vaul Later on, the construction of vaults became mor complicated. Three-segment vaults, star-shape vaults, and fan vaults appeared.

Arches also changed and became more com plex. A pointed arch could vary in both heigh and span. The narrowest arches were lance arches—pointed arches used on top of high narrow windows. Ogee arches were pointe arches that had a reversed curve near the top.

Another characteristic feature of Gothi architecture is the **flying buttress.** The flyin buttress consists of arched bars supported b massive stone columns set outside the walls of building. Flying buttresses were first full developed during the building of Notre Dam Cathedral in Paris.

Chartres Cathedral. 1194-1260. Chartres, France.
The perfection of the interior plan of the Chartres cathedral in France is the result of lessons learned from other buildings. There is no gallery, and the clerestory allows a lot of light into the nave. Three tiers of flying buttresses are a very important feature of Chartres.

As architectural design improved during the Middle Ages, walls ceased to be merely supports for a building. Architects began to put more imagination into building designs and arrangements.

Cathedrals were designed with four levels. At the bottom was the **nave.** Above it was the **gallery.** Above the gallery was the **triforium**, and topping them all was the **clerestory.**

Pillars, the inner shafts that supported the vaulting, became an important part of the cathedral design. Early pillars were cylindrical. The large pillars were often surrounded by several smaller pillars.

A cathedral is shaped like a cross. A central

nave running the length of the cathedral forms the main shaft of the cross. The nave is flanked by side aisles. The naves of the Gothic cathedrals are remarkable not only for their length, but also for their height. The higher the nave, the more light is allowed into the interior of the cathedral.

Two other important parts of a Gothic cathedral are the **apse** and the **transepts.** The apse is a

***Opposite*, Beauvais Cathedral. c. 1225-72. Beauvais, France.**
Cathedrals built after Chartres are examples of architectural brilliance. Architects searched for ways to make naves loftier and to replace walls with stained glass. Building methods were pushed to the limit. The architects of Beauvais in France made the nave walls almost 165 feet (50 meters) high. But these tall structures collapsed in 1284. Some of the cathedral was repaired and rebuilt, but the work was never finished. The collapse of the cathedral of Beauvais put an end to Gothic dreams of the gigantic.

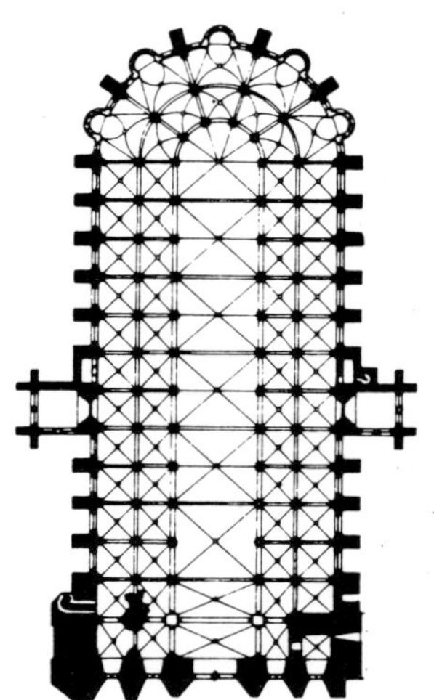

Ground plan of Bourges Cathedral. c. 1195. Bourges, France.
Gothic style and technical expertise in building reached its peak around 1190, about the time that the cathedrals of Bourges and Chartres were begun in France. The cathedral at Bourges followed a simple plan, similar to that of Notre Dame. The length of the cathedral's nave is unbroken by transepts. A double aisle surrounds the whole building.

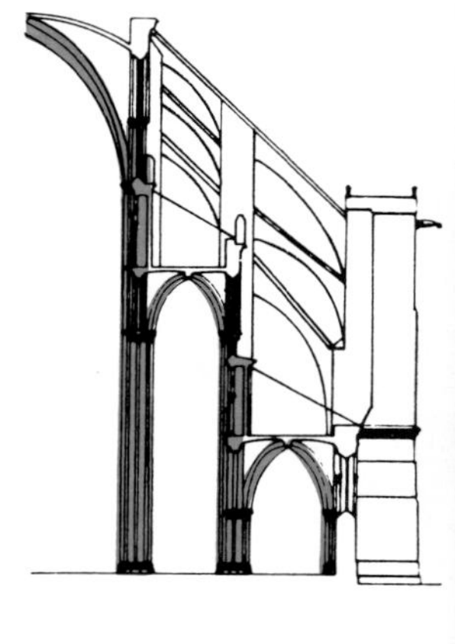

Cross-section of Bourges Cathedral. c. 1195. Bourges, France.
The architects at Bourges sought to give an impression of loftiness, as well as a sense of width and space in the cathedral. The intensity of light at the Bourges Cathedral cannot compare with that at the cathedral at Chartres. At Chartres, a single aisle channels the whole effect of the light into the nave.

semicircular area at the end of the nave. The apse is always at the east end of the nave and the entrance to the cathedral is always at the west. Transepts are sections of the building that project from both sides of the nave. The transepts form the horizontal crossbars of the cross design.

The apse design used in Gothic cathedrals was copied from early Romanesque churches. The apse in a cathedral is surrounded by an ambulatory and several side chapels that open out from the ambulatory.

Cathedral designs also included two towers on the western facade. These towers were often crowned with **spires.** The architectural plans of many cathedrals usually also called for other towers—up to a total of seven. In most cases, these towers were never completed or were finished centuries after the cathedral itself was completed.

A cathedral, dominating all other buildings around it, takes on a monumental dimension. The towering walls and the light streaming in

EVOLUTION OF TRACERY
Tracery is the ornamental stone ribbing and pattern work in the upper part of a Gothic window. The first Gothic windows were high, narrow, sharply-pointed windows known as lancet windows. These windows were crowned by a simple shape, either a three-parted leaf or a rose. Later, the designs became more complex and the stonework became more delicate.

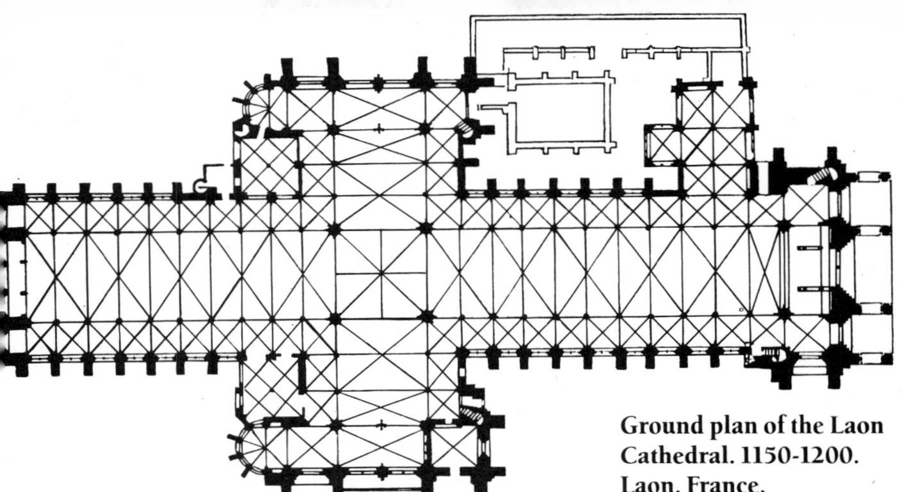

Ground plan of the Laon Cathedral. 1150-1200. Laon, France.
The cathedrals of Paris and Laon in France were built at the same time and share many details. Alterations at Laon have obscured some of the similarities between the two buildings, however. The original semicircular apse was replaced by a flat east end with huge windows. Six of the seven planned towers were built, though not all have spires.

hrough the windows seem to extend the rchitectural splendor downward to touch the veryday lives of the people.

The decoration and the arrangement of space nside a cathedral are very distinctive and reflect he thinking of the Gothic age. The writings of bbot Suger and his contemporaries refer to the nysticism of light. Light was seen as the mediator etween God and humanity. Therefore, one of he main goals of Gothic architecture was to eplace walls with stained glass windows. The

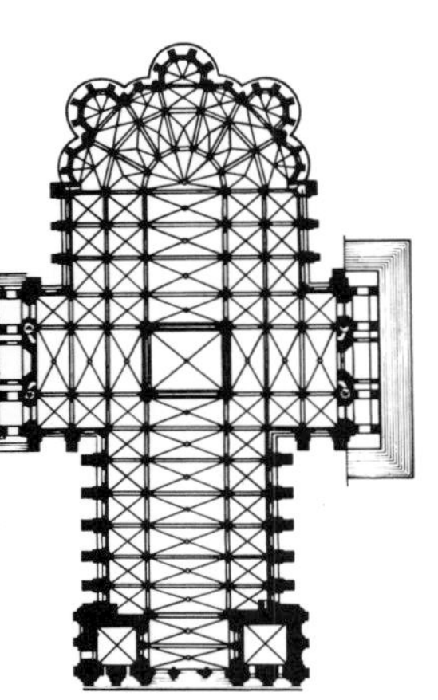

Ground plan of the Chartres Cathedral. 1194-1220. Chartres, France.
The cathedral at Chartres, considered one of the most perfect examples of a Gothic cathedral, served as a model for other cathedrals. The story of its building is typical of many cathedrals. When a fire in 1194 partially destroyed the old Romanesque cathedral on the site, the western facade was rebuilt. In 1334, another fire destroyed what remained of the old cathedral. Ambitious plans were drawn up for its reconstruction. The architect, wanting to preserve what had been built before, drew up his plans based on the old building. The newer west front, however, caused him to alter his plans.

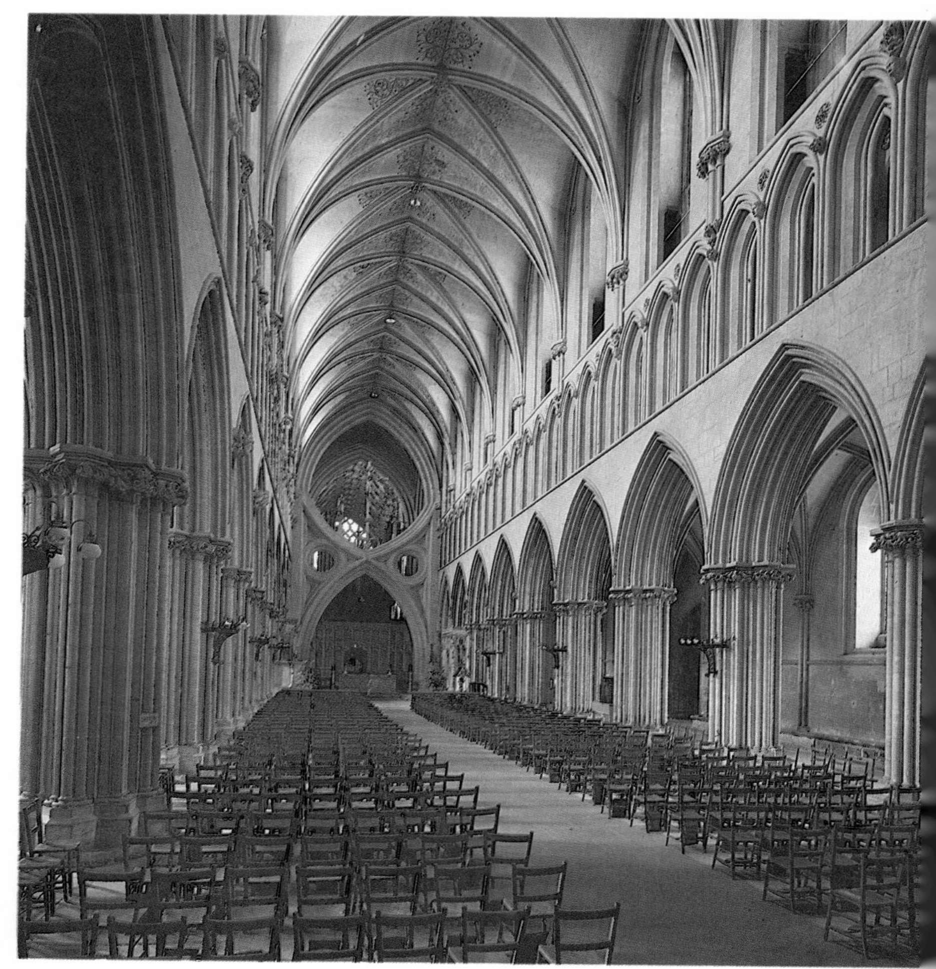

Nave. Wells Cathedral. 1214-1465. Wells, England.
The nave, the transepts, and the western bays of the church are designed in the Early English style—the first phase of English Gothic. When a great tower was added to the cathedral, the columns to support the tower had to be reinforced. This was accomplished by

builders wanted the light filtering through the stained glass to be evenly distributed. Light flooding in from above gave a sense of God's power from on high.

A discussion of Gothic architecture cannot be limited to cathedrals. Nor can it be limited to the story of the spread of the Gothic style from northern France across Europe.

Religious orders—particularly the Cistercians, Franciscans, and Dominicans—adapted the architecture of the age to suit their own particular

using inverted, pointed arches. These arches also give an extraordinary artistic look to this cathedral.

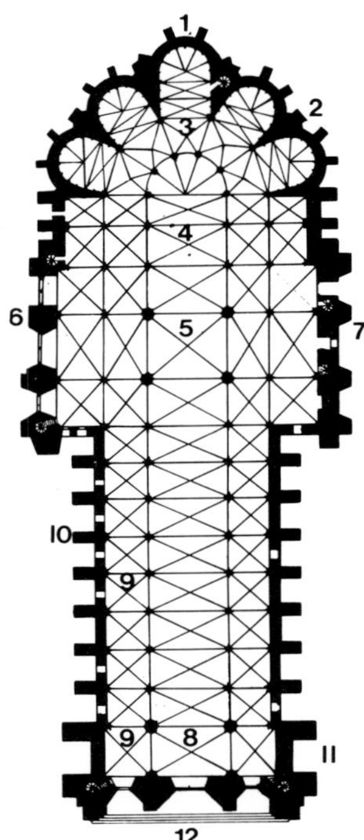

Ground plan of Reims Cathedral. 1212-41. Reims, France.
1. Apse 2. Chapels 3. Ambulatory 4. Presbytery 5. Crossing 6. North transept 7. South transept 8. Nave 9. Side aisles 10. Buttress 11. West end 12. Facade

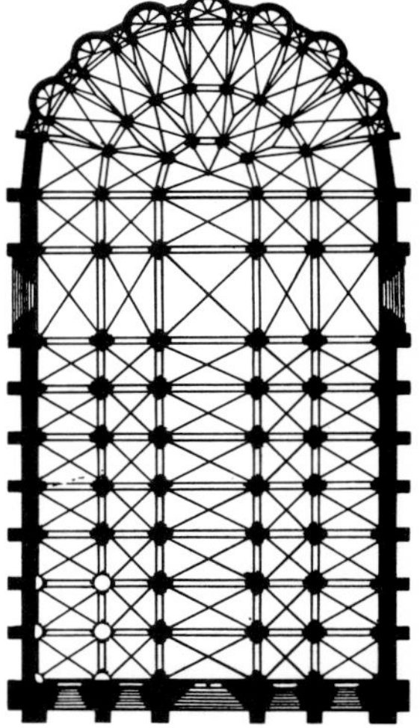

Ground plan of Toledo Cathedral. 1226. Toledo, Spain.
This five-aisle plan of the cathedral at Toledo is similar to the plans of Bourges and Notre Dame. There is a double ambulatory with two different types of chapels. The transepts do not stick out from the nave. Construction on the cathedral was begun by Archbishop Rodrigo Ximénez de Rada. He had visited Paris and was familiar with the cathedrals of that region. The first architect, Martin, may have been French, though he was followed by a local Spanish architect, Pedro Pérez.

needs. Though there were not specific "Cistercian" or "Franciscan" styles of Gothic architecture, the influence of these religious communities was powerful indeed.

The Cistercian order was founded at Citeaux in Burgundy in 1098. Saint Bernard, Abbot of Clairvaux, became a moving force in the order. He and his successors drew up rules that imposed great severity and simplicity on the abbey. There were to be no sculptures in the abbey's **porticos** (covered walkways), no stained glass in the windows, and no paintings within the monastery church.

The Cistercian order was not slow in taking part in the planning of royal buildings. The order took an active role in great building projects from Spain to eastern Europe. But the monumental buildings commissioned by the Cistercians were in complete contrast to the ideals of Saint Bernard.

Albi Cathedral. c. 1282. Albi, France.
Albi in France is a fortress church with impressive brick vaulting. The exterior is simple and solid. The internal space is huge. **Buttresses** (side supports) in the walls allow for many side chapels. Flamboyant-style additions built in the 1470s soften the cathedral's fortress-like aspects.

The Franciscans and the Dominicans flourished during the 13th century. Their founders, Saint Francis of Assisi and Saint Dominic, sought to revitalize the monastic spirit by preaching to people and spreading the Christian message. These orders proclaimed a new spirituality. They were more sensitive and more aware of the lives of ordinary people than were earlier religious orders. The teaching of the Franciscans and the Dominicans had an important effect upon art and literature.

Poverty was an essential part of the life of the Franciscans and the Dominicans. These groups established their monasteries in cities. By abandoning the agricultural life, they renounced the possession of land and the rents derived from land ownership.

For the design of their church buildings, both orders set up rules in keeping with their ideals of

Western facade. Strasbourg Cathedral. c. 1277. Strasbourg, France.
Strasbourg Cathedral in France was built in several stages and several styles, ending with the Radiant Gothic style on the west front. The tower of this cathedral rises into an **openwork** spire, 466 feet (142 m) high. The tower dates from around 1439 and is very representative of Germanic Gothic style.

poverty. As with the Cistercians, however, these general rules soon were broken. Their original goal was to keep decorations simple. But by the middle of the 13th century, some truly monumental buildings had been erected to hold large numbers of people. Within these buildings, the monks experimented with many interesting spacial effects—particularly large, undivided spaces.

The secular (non-religious) architecture of the

Nave. Gerona Cathedral. 14th century. Gerona, Spain.
This type of church, in which the nave is one vaulted hall, was introduced to Catalonia in Spain by the religious orders. Work started on the cathedral around 1312. When the first section had been built, doubts were raised about the width and solidity of the nave. After architects met in 1386 and 1416, they decided a single nave would result in a more solemn, better proportioned building and one in which there would be more light.

time is also very important, although civil buildings are less representative of the Gothic style than are religious buildings. In the civil buildings, practical considerations were more important than spiritual values. But civil architecture clearly reflects the nature of the society of the Middle Ages.

The most characteristic civil building is the palace, or aristocratic residence. The chief examples are the royal palaces, homes of the

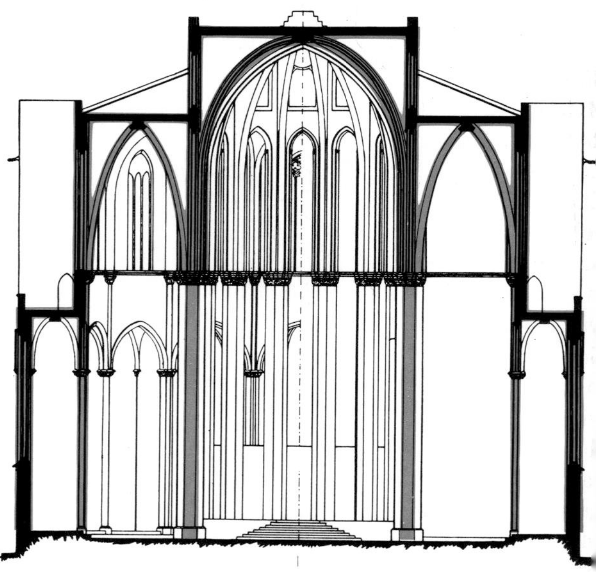

ruling monarchs. Not much remains of most of these palaces because changing tastes for comfort and splendor caused successive rulers to replace the Gothic-style buildings.

Another type of royal residence was the fortified castle. Some of the most spectacular castles are the Castel del Monte, built for Frederick II; the castle of Bellver, in Majorca; and the Castle of Karlstein, near Prague, built by the Emperor Charles IV.

The typical fortification plan consisted

ısically of a rectangular enclosure. The enclosure ıd towers and **turrets** on both sides and a **ɔnjon**, or massive inner tower, at the center.

The castle changed considerably during the othic period. It was originally built for defensive ırposes, but these became less important when udal leaders lost power to monarchs. When ıstles lost their military significance, many of ıem became luxurious residences.

In some countries, middle-class, urban dwellers

ERENGUER DE ONTAGUT and AMON DESPUIG. ross-section of the hurch of Santa Maria el Mar. c. 1328. ırcelona, Spain.

addition to churches ith a single, wide nave, ɔthic architects in Catalonia also built churches ith side aisles that were most as lofty as the central ave. One of these is the nta Maria del Mar church, hich was paid for by rich erchants of the town. ıe lack of ornamentation ustrates the purity of esign of this example of atalan Gothic architecture.

GIOTTO and others. Campanile. c. 1324. Florence Cathedral, Florence, Italy.

Giotto's activities as an architect should not be forgotten or considered secondary to his work as a painter. It is likely that Giotto supervised the building of Arena Chapel in Padua, as well as decorated the interior. He also designed the Campanile, or bell tower, for the cathedral in Florence, overseeing the work from 1334 until his death in 1337.

JUAN GUAS. Church of San Juan de los Reyes. 1477-1504. Toledo, Spain.
During the reign of Ferdinand and Isabella, a particular Gothic style developed in Spain. Called the Isabel style, it is characterized by its intricate decoration. The monastery of San Juan de los Reyes, which Ferdinand and Isabella founded, contains this chapel. It was built as a burial chapel. There is abundant decoration, but it does not intrude on the overall feeling of spaciousness. The single nave adds to this effect.

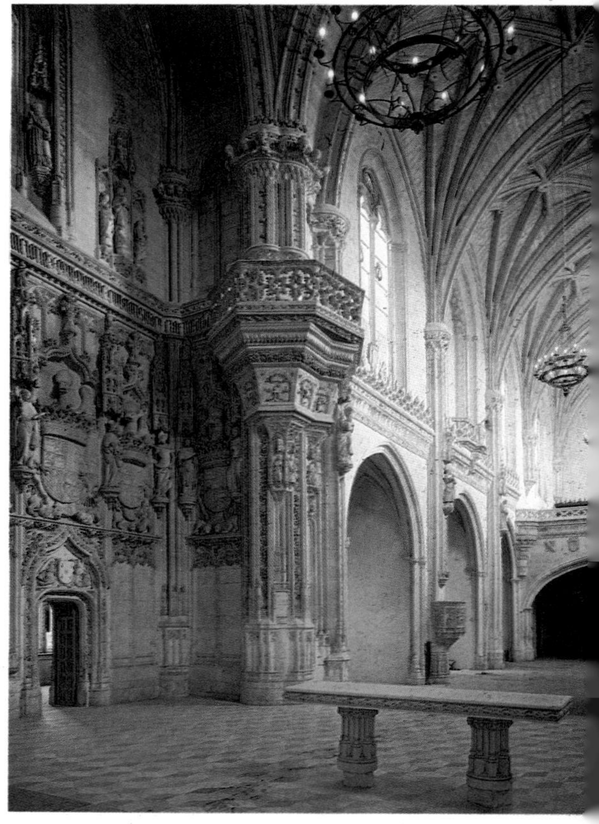

defied the power of the monarchy. They buil showy town halls as the seats of city governmen Such town halls are found in Florence and Sien in Italy, and in Brussels and Louvain in Belgiur The Casa de la Ciudada, in Barcelona, is perhap Spain's best example.

There were aristocratic mansions built in citie too. One example is the Palace of the Doges i Venice. In France, one of the best examples is th house of Jacques Coeur, a great merchant princ It has a fine courtyard and staircase tower.

Many European towns still retain parts of th medieval walls that once surrounded them. Thes walls served as physical and social boundarie

ilan Cathedral. 385-1416. Milan, Italy. Vork on this cathedral was lowed by controversy over ne bold design. Milan is ne second largest of the nedieval cathedrals. It s built entirely of white narble—even the flat roof is covered with marble slabs. Many leading European architects of the day were consulted on its design. The documents describing these consultations give a valuable insight into the planning and design of a cathedral. The exuberant decoration makes this cathedral very different from the architecture farther south in Italy.

or the townspeople. Often the legal status of hose living inside the town walls was totally lifferent from the status of those living outside.

Within the walls of a town, one found the mportant institutions of medieval life: the

ARNOLFO DI CAMBIO. Church of Santa Croce. c. 1295. Florence, Italy. The Church of Santa Croce, designed by Arnolfo di Cambio, is the finest example of a Franciscan Gothic church. The walls have no carving and are suitable for painted decoration. The Bardi and the Peruzzi chapels in the apse were decorated by Giotto. The church contains many richly decorated chapels—a far cry from the simplicity preached by Saint Francis.

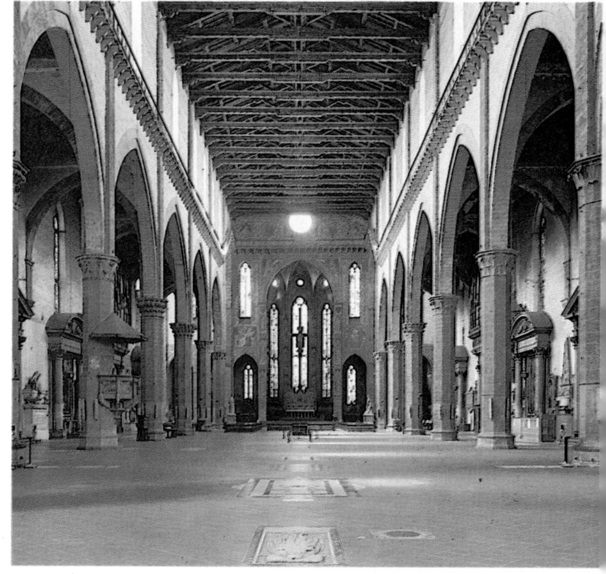

cathedral; the monasteries (usually at the outskirts of the town); and the palaces, guildhalls and hospitals. The degree of importance attached to these places determined the particular organization of each town.

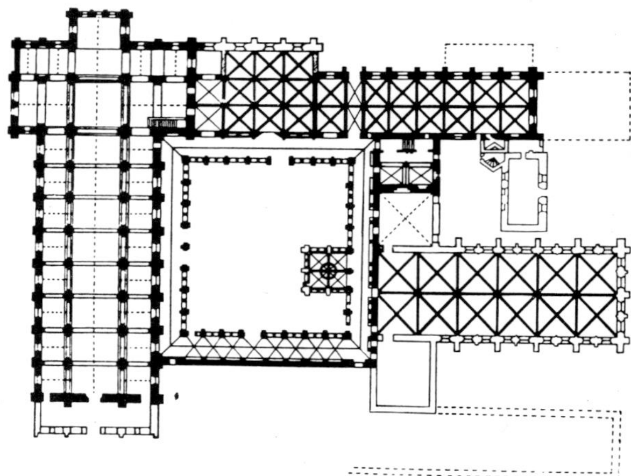

Ground plan of a Cistercian monastery. c. 1140. Fontenay, France. Monks from Clairvaux, where Saint Bernard was abbot, started to build the monastery of Fontenay, in Burgundy, around 1140. The buildings have survived almost intact and give us a very good idea of life within a Cistercian community. To the right of the church is the **cloister,** around which are grouped the library, the chapter (meeting) house, and the dormitory. The church is in the shape of a simple Latin cross.

GUILLEM SAGRERA. Exchange. 1426-51. Majorca, Spain.
Civic architecture in Aragon in northeast Spain assumed as much importance as religious architecture, possibly even more. When Sagrera began building the exchange in Majorca in 1426, his contract required that the work be completed in 12 years. However, when Sagrera left for Naples in 1477, the exchange was unfinished.

Most Gothic towns were linear, cross-shaped, or had streets radiating out from the center. Generally, these streets would curve around the boundaries of each quarter of the town. The main streets led to and from the town gates.

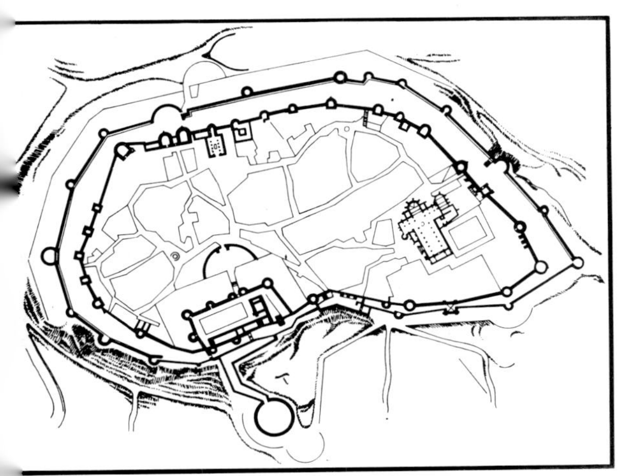

Citadel of Carcassonne. Late 13th century. Carcassonne, France.
Carcassonne, France, was the residence of the military governor of the surrounding conquered territories. The town was therefore fortified. Today Carcassonne is one of the best preserved of all medieval fortress towns. It had a double ring of walls. Within the walls, the Cathedral of Saint Nazario and the old castle are noteworthy. The street plan retains it medieval layout, even today.

Some documents describing town life during he period have survived. For the most part, the

Refectory of the Monastery of Santa Maria de Huerta. Early 13th century. Santa Maria de Huerta, Spain. Founded in the middle of the 12th century, the monastery of Huerta was once the most important monastery in Castile. It enjoyed royal protection. The refectory, or dining hall, is Gothic in design. The architect sought to emphasize the openness of the internal space by embedding features such as the staircase and lectern in the thickness of the walls. The ceiling has sexpartite (six-part) arches.

town was seen as an ideal place for the development of community and trade—and as a place in which to make one's fortune.

Sarmental Door. 1230-40. Burgos Cathedral, Burgos, Spain. The Sarmental Door, so called since it faces the vine market of the town (sarmiento means vine shoot), is the southern door of this cathedral. It is one of the oldest doors of the Castilian cathedrals. The central theme is the Apocalypse, with Christ shown in majesty. He is surrounded by the four evangelists, who are dressed as 13th-century scribes or clerks, and their symbols. The apostles appear on the lintel and an archbishop is depicted on the central column. The sharpness of the composition is typical of sculpture at the start of the Gothic period.

Gothic sculpture first appeared in the facades of the great cathedrals of the Île-de-France. In Romanesque doors, sculpture had been restricted to the **tympanum** and the **lintel**. But in Gothic doors, sculpture played an important part in the overall architectural design. This was another development of the Gothic style that began at the Abbey of Saint-Denis.

When Abbot Suger began the facade of his new abbey, his design included images of royalty as

ANONYMOUS.
***Horseman*. 13th century.**
Bamberg Cathedral,
Bamberg, West Germany.
Sculpture in the great cathedrals of the Germanic world developed from the style begun at Reims, but became less graceful and lifelike and displayed more angular forms. No longer confined to facades, sculpture began to blossom inside churches. Portraits of princes and nobles were commonly carved on pillars. Some historians believe the rider shown here was a member of the imperial family. Others believe him to be one of the three kings who traveled to worship young Jesus.

well as images of the saints. Kings, queens, and figures from the Old Testament were grouped together on what became known as the Royal Doorway. There was obviously a desire to enhance the image of the king and to give him a greater aura of royal dignity.

At Saint-Denis, columnar-statues—columns with almost free-standing portrait statues carved on them—appear for the first time. With the appearance of columnar-statues, monumental sculpture began to break free from its minor role as part of the architecture of a building. The statues were not merely an addition to the

ANONYMOUS. *The Annunciation*. Late 13th century. Reims Cathedral, Reims, France.
Reims Cathedral, despite the bombardments it suffered during World War I, still possesses an extensive variety of Gothic sculpture. This sculpture from above the central doorway illustrates the variety of sculptural form and style found at the cathedral. The image of Mary is from an earlier period than that of the angel. The Virgin's stiff pose contrasts greatly with the elegant lines of the gentle, smiling angel. The figures seem to be independent of the structure of the building itself.

building, but rather a sculptural extension of it. This new harmony between architecture and sculpture was the starting point for the great Gothic doorways.

During the early 13th century, work began on the doorways of the great cathedrals that had been started in the previous century—Laon, Chartres, Paris, Amiens, Bourges, and Reims. The Royal Doorway at Chartres (1145-55) was modeled on the Saint-Denis doorway both in structure and in the way the saints are depicted. Its magnificence lies in the clarity with which the various themes are portrayed.

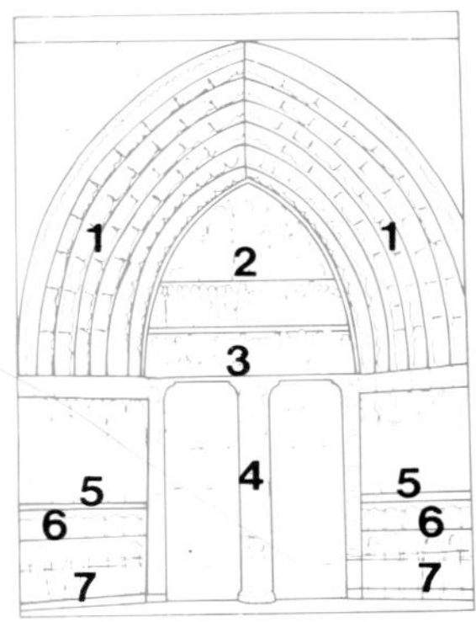

Architectural points of a doorway
1. Archivaults 2. Tympanum 3. Lintel 4. Central column 5. Statues or column-figures 6. Jambs 7. Plinth or Pedestal

CLAUS SLUTER.
***Moses's Well.* 1395-99.**
Carthusian monastery at Champmol, Dijon, France.
Sluter considered sculpture to be separate from a building. In this sculpture, Moses and other Old Testament prophets surround a symbolic well. The decorative effect of this sculpture is enhanced by the sheer exuberance of the draperies on the figures. The Carthusian house at Champmol in France was chosen by the Dukes of Burgundy as the burial place of their dynasty. This explains the building's superb decoration.

The sculptures on these doorways are more refined than were those on Romanesque cathedrals. Figures were positioned to suggest a certain liveliness. They tended to be smaller, more lifelike, and less exaggerated in length than those created in the Romanesque era. The shape of the human body could be spotted beneath the figures' clothing, and realistic expressions, such as the characteristic smile, appeared on faces of the sculpted figures.

The Last Judgment is a theme used often in the central tympanum of the Gothic doorways. The scene shows a suffering but triumphant Christ from the Gospel according to Saint Matthew. Christ bears the wounds of the crucifixion and is surrounded by characters associated with the Passion. The lintels usually show the separation of the blessed from the damned. The arches are adorned with choirs of angels and other figures.

A representation of Christ might occupy the central column of the Gothic doorway, though this space was usually reserved for an image of the Virgin Mary.

The cult of the Virgin is a characteristic of

ANONYMOUS. *Charles V.* 1364-80. The Louvre, Paris, France.
During the reign of Charles V, some of the problems that beset European society in the 14th century were beginning to be felt. Yet the art of Charles's court remained perfect and refined. This statue of Charles, which was paired with one of his wife, Jeanne de Bourbon, illustrates some of the essentials of Gothic sculpture from the 14th century. It is one of the earliest portrait statues. The sculptor sought to show the king as a kind, fatherly person. Portrait statues became more popular during the 14th century due to the great number of patrons and donors willing to pay to be immortalized in sculpture.

NICOLA PISANO.
***The Birth of Christ*. 1260. Pulpit in the baptistery, Pisa Cathedral, Pisa, Italy.**
The inspiration for Nicola Pisano's style came from southern Italy, where Emperor Frederick II encouraged works that imitated the art of ancient Rome. Pisano's first great work, in which many classical influences can be seen, was this pulpit in the baptistry at Pisa Cathedral. But the quality of human feeling is unmistakably Gothic.

GIOVANNI PISANO.
***The Massacre of the Innocents*. 1301. Pulpit of the Church of Saint Andrew, Pistoia, Italy.**
Pulpits are among the works that best illustrated the beginnings of Gothic sculpture in Italy. Giovanni Pisano, son of Nicola Pisano, carved the pulpits in the Pisa Cathedral and this church in Pistoia. In contrast to the classical style of his father's work, Giovanni tried to bring out the dramatic and emotional aspects of his subject. It has been said that his sculpture was influenced by French marble works. Pisano himself produced many excellent works in marble. The figure of Herod,

Gothic art. It was particularly encouraged by the Cistercian order. The Virgin was often represented on the main or side panels of the tympanum at the moment of her coronation.

Originally, the **jambs**—upright pieces forming the sides of the door—displayed crowned figures that gave the name "royal" to the doorways. These figures were gradually replaced by images of apostles or saints. It is also not unusual to find the figure of an archbishop in the place of honor on the central column.

The elements forming these doorways are an integral part of the facade of the cathedral. The

in the top right corner, leads this dramatic episode. Though at first glance the composition seems confused, the figures do follow a series of diagonal lines. Like Giotto, Pisano knew how to compose his sculpture based on pictorial methods.

ANDREA PISANO. *Baptism of Christ*. 1330. Doors of the baptistery, Florence Cathedral, Florence, Italy.
Andrea Pisano brought a feeling of reality to his sculpture. His best known works are the magnificent bronze doors of the baptistery at the Florence Cathedral. The scenes depicted are from the life of Saint John the Baptist. Each scene is enclosed in its own panel and contains just enough detail to make its theme clear.

gables and **pinnacles** that crown the doors are linked to the galleries and upper sections of the building. In some cases, the galleries housed additional sculptures. Sometimes the doorways projected outward, forming a type of porch.

These 13th-century doorways made the lives and stories of the saints more widely known. They also presented an opportunity for sculpture "in the round." Whereas Romanesque sculpture took the form of **relief** carvings on buildings, Gothic sculpture was almost free-standing and independent of the architectural elements of the building. The separation of sculpture from architecture was a new and important advance.

Compared to the monumental works of earlier centuries, French architecture of the 14th century is full of small buildings. Sculpture was used in a much freer form. The figures often seem to have no connection with the building itself.

The cathedrals of Siena and Orvieto were under construction around 1300. Though the buildings were based largely on French models, the sculptures were used in an original way. Instead of being confined to the jambs and vaulted arches, the sculptures are attached to the walls themselves. At Siena, the characters designed by Giovanni Pisano stand out from the wall and have great movement and expression. At Orvieto, the sculptures are on the pillars that separate each of the doors.

Sculptured decoration is also given a great deal of space inside Gothic cathedrals and churches. Sculpture is usually found around the presbytery. In French cathedrals, a screen called the **rood screen** divided the space reserved for the clergy and the choir from the rest of the church. Many of these screens have richly carved sculptural decoration.

In Italy, the pulpit became the chief object for

MICHAEL PACHER. *Coronation of the Virgin.* 1471-81. Parish church, Saint Wolfgang, Austria. Engraved and carved altarpieces are some of the best examples of late Gothic sculpture in Germany and the Low Countries. Many altarpieces are exquisite. They usually consist of a central piece, with fully rounded sculptures, and two hinged side panels that can be closed. The interior surfaces of the panels are carved in relief, and the exteriors or backs of the panels are painted. In the Low Countries, altarpieces were mass produced in workshops, almost on an assembly line system. In Germany, the pieces were individually carved by masters. The piece shown here is considered to be Pacher's finest work. The abundance of gilded and decorative elements does not detract from the order and control of the whole piece.

othic sculptural decoration. In Spain, the pulpit 'as usually situated in the middle of the **choir,** in ıe center of the nave. This positioning allowed ıe display of marvellous rood screens made of ırved wood. The walls of the choir were often overed with magnificent sculpture, some of it of ıonumental proportions.

Another area in which sculpture took hold and ourished was in the **altarpieces**—carvings, often ıade of wood, that decorated the space behind ıe altars. It was not until the 15th century that ıese altarpieces became truly monumental, specially in the Low Countries (Belgium, uxembourg, and the Netherlands) and Germany.

Throughout Spain there are a great many ltarpieces made of stone or alabaster. These eached the peak of their splendor in the 15th entury. The stone pieces, heavier than the 'ooden sculptures of the north, focused attention n the presbytery.

ANTOINE LE MOITURIER. Tomb of Phillip Pot. c. 1480. The Louvre, Paris, France. Mourners—almost life size—give a monumental dimension to this tomb carving. The funereal impression is heightened by the flowing black robes and hoods that hide the mourner's faces. The tomb was at the Cistercian abbey at Citeaux.

GIL DE SILOE. Tomb of the Crown Prince Alfonso. 1489-93. Miraflores Monastery, Burgos, Spain. Gil de Siloe, a Flemish sculptor, completed several impressive works in the Miraflores Monastery. He created the altarpiece, the tomb shown here, and the tombs of the founders of the monastery—Juan II of Castile and Isabel of Portugal. The delicate alabaster tomb is representative of the exquisite work of Flemish and German artists who lived in Spain at the end of the 15th century. The crown prince is depicted on his knees, dressed in rich robes, looking toward the high altar.

Funeral monuments express better thar anything else the attitude toward life and deatl in Gothic society. Such monuments also reveal the need for certain individuals to be rememberec after their death. During the Gothic period funeral rites acquired more and more socia significance and became increasingly solemn Funeral chapels and tombs became widespreac and achieved a monumental dignity.

In these monuments, a statue of the deceased sually appears lying on the coffin, though the erson may also be shown praying, meditating, r reading. Sometimes the person is depicted as sleep or dead, often with an expression hinting : the pain of death. The figure would be dressed s suited his position in life—a bishop would be nown in church robes and nobles would wear rmor or military outfits. Royalty might be shown n robes representing their royal state or their nembership in a religious order.

There are many types of Gothic funeral nonuments. Sometimes burial places—particu- rly the tombs of saints or royalty—were set part in a funeral chapel. In special cases, a tomb ecame a sort of public monument. More equently, tombs were placed in arched en- losures within church walls.

One recurring theme of tomb decoration is hat of hooded figures in flowing robes. These vere mourners shown in various dramatic poses.

There are also devotional images in tomb ecoration. Intense, dramatic images of Christ rucified, and softer images showing the elationship between the Virgin and Child are he most widespread. Themes such as the rucifixion and the burial of Christ are ntentionally dramatized in order to appeal to he emotions of the faithful.

ANONYMOUS.
***Christ Crucified*. c. 1307.**
Perpignan Cathedral, Perpignan, France.
Emotion is one of the dominant characteristics of Gothic imagery. The Virgin

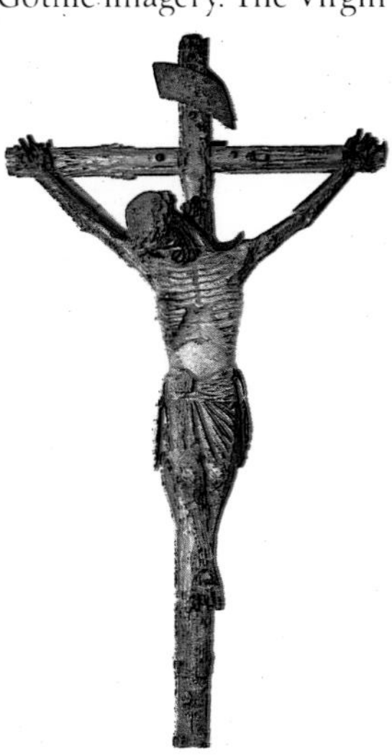

is shown as a real mother. The crucified Christ is shown with compassion intended to affect the emotions of the onlooker.

Duce-
bant
tur autem cum
ihu duo lat-
nes ut crucifi-
gerentur et post-
quam venerunt
ad locum qui
dicitur cal-
varie: ibi
crucifixerunt
eum.

Duo la-
trones
duos populos
significant iudeo-
rum scilicet et gen-
tium qui mor-
ti eterne addic-
ti erant per pec-
catum ade per quod
solvendo ihc
cruci clavis
affixus erat.
et per hoc osten-
ditur quam
magnum fuit
peccatum ade:
quando manum
ad arborem ve-
titam exten-
dit.

Milites ergo
cum cru-
cifixissent eum:
diviserunt sibi
vestimenta eius
et fecerunt iiii
partes unicui-
que militi
partem. Super
tunicam que erat
inconsutilis
desuper contexta
per totum: sortem
mittebant.

Quadri-
partita
vestis: significat
ecclesiam in qua-
tuor partibus
orbis diffu-
sam. omnibus
partibus eius tribu-
id est concorditer dis-
tributam. Tu-
nica sortita:
omnium patrum
significat unita-
tem quam uno
caritatis vin-
culo continet.

Et imposuerunt
super caput eius
causam ipsius scrip-
tam ihc naza-
renus rex iudeorum.
Erat autem scrip-
tum hebraice
grece et latine.
Contradicebant
ergo pylato pon-
tifices iudeorum.
Respondit pi-
latus. Quod
scripsi scripsi.

Quod in
morte
ihu ascribeba-
tur ei titulus
triumphalis:
significat quod in fi-
ne penitentie
sue regnabit
quilibet vere
penitens cum
xpo. Quod iudei
contradixerunt
scripture et pilatus
confirmavit: sig-
nificat quod iudei
fidei xpi contra-
dixerunt. sed pa-
gani eam admi-
serunt et retinue-
runt.

Tunc cruci
fixi sunt cum
eo duo latrones
unus a dextris et alter
a sinistris. Unus autem
de hiis blasphe-
mabat eum dicens.
Si tu es xpc: sal-
vum fac temet
ipsum et nos. Res-
pondens alter
increpabat eum.
et dicebat ad ihe-
sum. Domine me-
mento mei dum
veneris in regnum
tuum. et dixit ei
ihc. Amen dico tibi:
hodie mecum eris
in paradiso.

Per latro-
nem qui
a dextris erat.
significantur ve-
re penitentes qui
carnem suam cruci
figunt cum viciis et
concupiscentiis pro
celestibus. Quod per dexte-
ram significantur. per
latronem a sinistris
significantur ypocrite qui
opera prave agunt
et vivunt sed pro temporali-
bus.

PAINTING

Moral Bible. Late 13th century. Toledo Cathedral, Toledo, Spain. One of the principal groups of miniaturists active in Paris during the reign of Saint Louis specialized in the production of these Bibles. This example, given by Louis IX to Alfonso the Wise, is kept in the Toledo Cathedral. These books consist of biblical passages, graphically illustrated, to form complete histories. The miniatures, which in this case refer to the Crucifixion, have little perspective or depth and are arranged to resemble the stained glass windows found in churches of the time.

In the field of manuscript illumination a distinct style began to emerge. Around the year 1200, a very definite Byzantine influence appeared. It was marked by a flowing style that gives a feeling of great vitality to the scenes depicted.

As the 13th century progressed, illumination became more important. Cathedral schools and universities demanded more books. These books could no longer be written in the monasteries, but were produced in specialized workshops set up in the growing European towns.

Royalty, too, began to show a great interest in books. But they desired a different type of book than those made during the Romanesque period. Earlier books had been used in monastic communities. Many of the books of the Gothic age were for private devotion. They were mainly Psalters (collections of psalms) and private prayer books called "Books of Hours." Books of a non-religious nature were produced as well.

Paris became the center for the production of splendid manuscripts, mostly designed and produced for the French monarchs. During the reign of Louis IX (1226-70), exceptional works

ANONYMOUS. Panels from the tomb of Sancho Sáiz de Carrillo. c. 1300. Museum of Catalan Art, Barcelona, Spain.
In these tomb paintings, grief-stricken men and women tear their hair. The intensity of the theme is increased by the mourners' gestures and by the linear style of drawing. The technique used—the paintings were done on parchment and then fixed to the panel—resembles the work of the miniaturists.

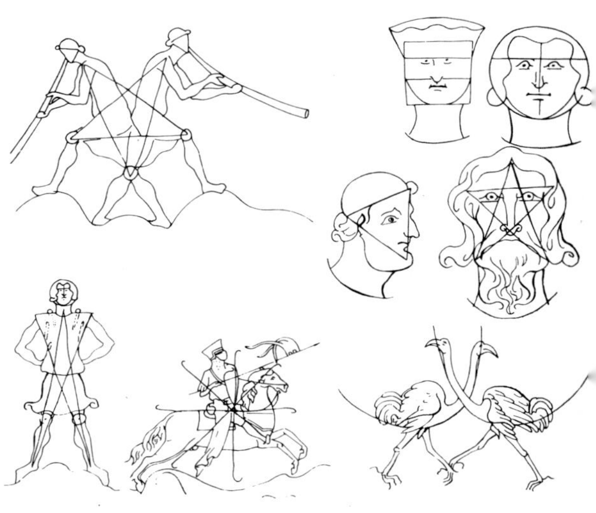

VILLARD DE HONNECOURT. Studies in Proportion. Early 13th century. National Library, Paris, France.
Villard de Honnecourt's book contains many notes referring to technical points about drawing. His studies of proportion are reproduced here. From these drawings it is possible to understand how artists

were produced. At the end of the 13th centur miniatures often featured elongated figures o backgrounds of gold and enclosed in stylize frameworks.

Gothic mural (wall) painting developed i southern Europe. As the Gothic style develope the Italians began to search for ways to combin Gothic architecture and wall painting. A perfec match was found when buildings, until the shown merely as backgrounds *behind* the figure in a painting, became an integral part of th compositions.

When the Italian painters began to plac their figures inside architectural settings, the

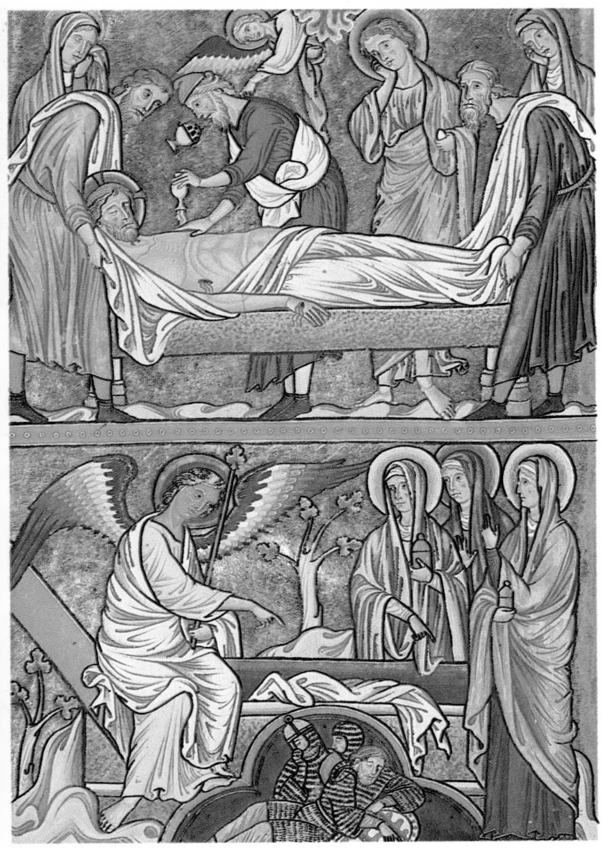

of the Gothic period saw the human body. The artists were trying to break down the human form into geometrical shapes as a basis for later stylization.

Psalter of Queen Ingeburge. c. 1200. Musée Condé, Chantilly, France.
This Psalter (book of psalms) belonged to Queen Ingeburg, second wife of Phillipe Auguste of France (1180-1223). It was one of the earliest of the ornate books made for the French court and was probably illustrated by miniaturists from the north of France. They may have had contacts with English miniaturists, for the Byzantine influence that was widespread in England at the time is very evident in the depiction of the saints. The framing of each scene and the gold backgrounds are similar to Byzantine mosaic work.

undertook the first exercises in **perspective.** This resulted in greater clarity in painting and was a great step forward in the art of representational painting.

The decoration of the high altar at Assisi is an example of this combination of art and architecture. The painting enriches the entire building and has an intimate relationship with the architecture. It is unclear who actually painted it. It may have been Giotto, who was also director of the architectural work at Assisi.

Giotto's principal work was the decoration of the Arena Chapel at Padua (1304-06). It is clear that this work was designed and executed by one

GIOTTO. ***Joachim Expelled from the Temple.*** **1304-06. Arena Chapel, Padua, Italy.**
Giotto's paintings cover all the walls of this Italian chapel. They are mainly scenes from the life of Christ and the Virgin. Though at first sight the paintings appear confusing, a feeling of order soon prevails. The paintings are composed for a viewer who is assumed to be standing in the middle of the chapel. This picture is the first in a narrative cycle, a series of pictures that tell a story. The architecture of the temple stands out against the blue background but is reduced to a minimum to emphasize the action of the figures.

person, with very little assistance. The simplicity of the paintings and their reflection of the austere lines of the building lead art historians to the conclusion that Giotto must have had a hand in the construction of the chapel itself.

GIOTTO. *The Marriage at Canaa in Galilee.* 1304-06. Arena Chapel, Padua, Italy.
This diagram of Giotto's painting shows the typical composition used by the artist. The scene is set in a building that opens out like the front of a doll's house. The side walls give an impression of depth because of their slanted angle. The depth is emphasized by the L-shaped table and the positioning of figures and objects around it. The perspective is not scientifically accurate, but it does provide greater pictorial clarity to the scene.

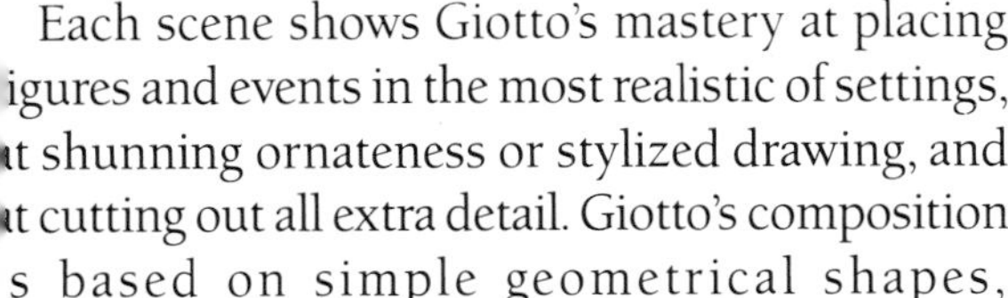

Each scene shows Giotto's mastery at placing igures and events in the most realistic of settings, ıt shunning ornateness or stylized drawing, and ıt cutting out all extra detail. Giotto's composition s based on simple geometrical shapes,

DUCCIO DI BUONINSEGNA. *Majesty.* 1308-11. Cathedral Museum, Siena, Italy. The front of this work shows the Virgin Mary in all her majesty, surrounded by angels and saints. It is in the Byzantine tradition and has a monumental effect. On the reverse panels there is an extensive narrative cycle based on the Passion. The artist's style is similar to that used by mural painters, yet it shows the delicacy demanded for painting on panels. The work commanded a very high price.

emphasized by architectural features that open out to give space to the scenes.

It has been said that the works of Giotto and his followers were creations at the very edge of Gothic art, or were even early examples of Renaissance art. They are considerably ahead of their time, but they are definitely of the Gothic period.

As important as Giotto was, Duccio di Buoninsegna was no less important. He worked mainly in Siena, where he painted on **panels.** The new style of expression used on the walls of the church at Assisi is found in Duccio's altarpieces. Duccio's work has a great degree of exuberance.

Italian painting evolved from the new use of the perspective it had introduced. The Italian painters eventually created a new vision of the

JUAN OLIVER. Paintings in the refectory of Pamplona Cathedral, 1330. Diocesan Museum, Pamplona, Spain. These paintings—signed and dated 1330—show Gothic artists beginning to move away from simple linear design. Color is also becoming more important than it had been in earlier works. This central scene shows Christ crucified with three nails. Christ's suffering is emphasized by the abundant blood flowing from his wounds. The blood accomplishes its redemptive role when it reaches Adam's skull at the foot of the cross. To the right are shown the Jewish people, and to the left are Saint John with the holy women.

ANONYMOUS. *Pentecost*. Fragment of an altarpiece. c. 1347. Narodny Gallery, Prague, Czechoslovakia. After his coronation, Emperor Charles IV took up residence in Prague, Czechoslovakia. He turned the city into one of the most important artistic centers of the day. Much of the city was rebuilt and painters and sculptors were at work everywhere. Bohemian art was much influenced by Italian models. This altarpiece is believed to have been created by a group of artists working directly for the emperor.

CONSTRUCTION OF AN ALTARPIECE

The altarpiece acquired monumental dignity during the Gothic period. It could consist of a painting, a work in precious metal, or a sculpture. It was

world embodied by the Renaissance. The French court, on the other hand, retained established artistic values in painting. Though elements of Italian art were borrowed by the French, they were treated very stylistically.

In the **miniatures** by Jean Pucelle—especially those found in Jeanne d'Evreux's Book of Hours—golden backgrounds give way to architectural backgrounds. The architectural backgrounds appear to be directly inspired by Duccio's work. Pucelle's miniatures have some of the traits of

traditionally divided into sections horizontally and vertically. Usually it was surrounded by a dust guard and was often crowned by pinnacles, or spires.

SIMONE MARTINI. *The Road to Calvary*. c. 1340. The Louvre, Paris, France. Painting done in Siena continued the style established by Duccio—especially in the way the human figure was portrayed with tenderness and emotion. Simone Martini began working in Siena and contributed to the international spread of this style of painting. The work shown here forms part of a **polyptych**—an arrangement of four or more hinged panels. The intensity of color and attention to detail link this work closely to the miniature style. The work did indeed directly influence some miniaturist painters.

Dominica resurrectionis domi
ni. Ad matutinum. Invitatorium.
Surrexit dominus vere alleluia.
Ps. Venite. Hymni et capi
tula non dicuntur in aliqua ho
ra usque ad vesperas sabbati nec ver
siculi nisi ad nocturnum. Ad N.
Ego sum qui sum et
consilium meum non est
cum impiis sed in lege domini vo
luntas mea est alleluia. Ps. Bea
tus vir. A. Postulavi patrem meum
alleluia dedit michi gentes alleluia in
hereditatem alleluia. Ps. Quare
fremuerunt. A. Ego dormivi
et somnum cepi et exsurrexi quoniam
dominus suscepit me alleluia alleluia.

V. Surrexit dominus de sepul
chro alleluia. R. Qui pro nobis pe
pendit in ligno alleluia.
In illo tem- Secundum
pore: Maria marcum.
a magdalene et mari
a iacobi et salome a
beuntes emerunt aro
mata ut venientes unge
rent ihesum. Et reliqua. Omelia
beati gregorii pape de eadem lectione.
Audistis fratres lectio prima
karissimi quod sancte muli
eres que dominum secute fuerant
cum aromatibus ad mo
numentum venerunt et ei
quem viventem dilexerant
etiam mortuo studio huma

100

4th-century illuminated manuscripts. Pucelle chieved harmony between text and image by ne ornamentation of initial letters and by ecoration in the margins of the manuscripts.

pposite, JEAN UCELLE. Breviary of eanne d'Evreux. c. 1330. lusée Condé, Chantilly, rance.
his breviary, or prayer book, cannot compare in excellence with the Jeanne d'Evreux's Book of Hours. Pucelle used **grisaille**, painting with tones of a single color, which gave the effect of sculpture to his figures. This page features decoration in the margin and pictures interspersed with the text. These elements are typical of the 13th-century miniaturists. In contrast with the abundant golden backgrounds in some books, the restricted range of colors used here emphasizes the delicacy of the style.

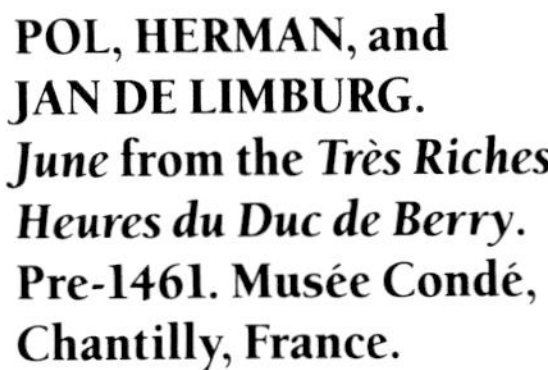

POL, HERMAN, and JAN DE LIMBURG. *June* from the *Très Riches Heures du Duc de Berry*. Pre-1461. Musée Condé, Chantilly, France.
If any of the miniatures in this exquisite book stand out, it is those illustrating the months of the calendar. The labor of the month of June is shown with little or no perspective. The scene takes place in a countryside dominated by recognizable castles. The harvest is gathered in front of the royal palace on the far bank of the Seine in France. The church on the right is the Sainte Chapelle. The contrast between the simplicity of rural life and the aristocratic castle is typical of the style of the time. The traditional golden background has been replaced by a bright blue sky. The raised viewpoint gives some feeling of depth to the landscape.

JAN and HUBERT VAN EYCK. Polyptych of the Sacrificial Lamb. Center panel. 1432. Cathedral of Saint Bavon, Ghent, Belgium.
An inscription on the outside of this wonderful piece states that it was made jointly by the brothers Hubert and Jan van Eyck. It is said that no one surpassed Hubert's skill as a painter, though his brother was said to be a close second. Historians are not sure which parts of this polyptych were painted by which brother. The center panel is dominated by the vision of omnipotent God, together with the Virgin and Saint John. The lower panel represents the adoration of the lamb. In front of the altar on which the lamb stands is the fountain of life with crowds of saints and biblical characters moving toward it.

The peak of Gothic miniature painting was reached at the court of Jean, Duc de Berry. His passion for collecting books led him to fill a library with splendid manuscripts and to commission Books of Hours from well-known artists with varied styles.

An "international" Gothic style developed and it dominated European courts until around 1400.

JAN VAN EYCK. *The Arnolfini Marriage*. 1434. National Gallery, London, England.
Giovanni Arnolfini was an Italian businessman who lived in Bruges with his wife, Giovanna Cenami. The couple are shown in a room full of objects that reflect their everyday life—the dog, the wooden clogs Arnolfini wears to avoid the filth in the streets, the fruit bowl, and, above all, the mirror on the wall. The mirror serves as an unusual pictorial device, showing

s other persons present
ı the room. The artist has
ıgned the work "Jan van
yck was here." Within this

simple scene are many symbolic references to the sacredness of marriage. The hiding of symbolism in reality was one of the principles of Gothic painting that Flemish artists used extensively.

BARTOLOMÉ BERMEJO. *Saint Dominic of Silos.* 1474-77. Prado Museum, Madrid, Spain.
The abundance of decoration that characterizes late Spanish Gothic work is clearly shown on this altarpiece. The saintly abbot in his robes is solemn, but this does not disguise the deep humanity shining out from his face. Each tiny detail is carefully treated, revealing some of the techniques developed by the Flemish painters. The figures above the throne add a touch of color and liveliness to this impressive picture.

HANS MEMLING. *The Holy Women.* Late 15th century. Royal Chapel, Granada, Spain.
During the 14th and 15th centuries, kings and queens in Europe collected many precious objects. At first these were valued for their exotic or luxurious nature. But they soon came to be appreciated as works of art. Thus were formed the beginnings of great art collections. Ferdinand and Isabella of Spain collected many manuscripts, books, jewels, tapestries, and

In this style, the stiffness of earlier Gothic art is softened by the natural feeling introduced by the Italian painters. However, while the Italians painted a simple reality, northern European courts preferred an exotic reality, full of contrasts and detail.

ıbove all, paintings. Standing apart from the rest of he paintings are those by 'lemish artists. One of the finest is the diptych (a picture on two hinged panels) of which this scene is a part. The painting is notable for the impression of grief that it conveys, the placing of the figures, and the background.

This contradiction is obvious in Flemish painting —work produced in the towns and cities of Belgium— during the 15th century.

A new technique—oil painting—perfected by Flemish artists allowed painters to capture detail in a way far superior to that of the miniaturists. The new technique allowed artists to obtain previously undreamed-of effects of light and color. The final effect of the Flemish work was nevertheless unrealistic, partly because of the lack of movement and the heavy symbolism in the paintings.

JAUME HUGUET. *Saint George and the Princess.* c. 1445. Museum of Catalan Art, Barcelona, Spain.
This image of Saint George, attributed to Jaume Huguet, seems to have been the center panel of a triptych. (The two side panels are in the Berlin Museum.) Saint George, dressed as a gentleman of the time, is portrayed elegantly. There is something of the international Gothic style about this painting, mixed with a certain Italian air. This is probably one of Huguet's early works. His later style was very much influenced by the tastes of his clients, who preferred shiny golden backgrounds to scenery. The extraordinary humanity and the vague sadness of the figures are the main interest in Huguet's pictures.

LUÍS BORRASSÀ.
he Fall of the Antichrist.
416. Panel from the tarpiece in the Church Saint Michael at cruilles. Museum of Art, erona, Spain.

Borrassà was one of the great fans of the international Gothic style in Catalonia. Extensive records detail his life and busy artistic activity. This is one of the outstanding scenes from the altarpiece, one of Borrassà's later works. The gold background emphasizes the unreal and fantastic nature of the scene.

ROGER VAN DER WEYDEN. ***Descent from the Cross.*** **c. 1436. Prado Museum, Madrid, Spain.** Just as Jan van Eyck gave his paintings a very symmetrical, or balanced, appearance that tends to make them static, so Roger van der Weyden is known for the rhythm he conveyed. This work is a good example of that rhythm. The parallel positions of Christ and the Virgin are intended to show the feeling of compassion so dear to the Gothic spirit. This scene, almost sculptural within its closed frame, is the central panel of a triptych.

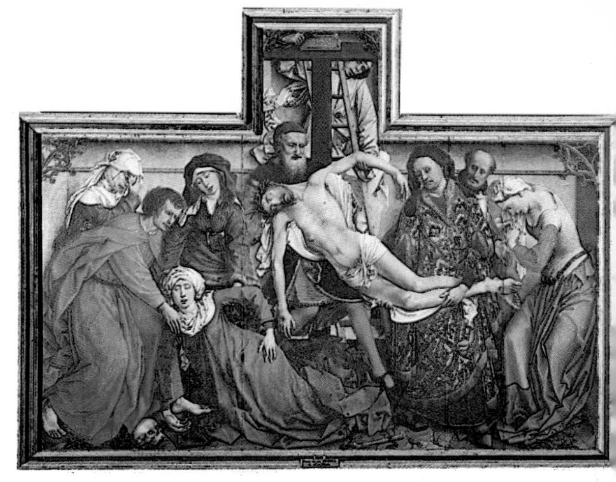

Jan van Eyck produced many masterpieces in which he shows his great artistic sensitivity. He used modern treatments of light, space, and perspective and was one of the first Gothic painters to develop the portrait as a likeness of the sitter. He also put forth the idea of a picture being the work of a specific painter.

KONRAD WITZ. ***The Miraculous Draught of Fishes.*** **1444. Museum of Art and History, Geneva, Switzerland.** The altarpiece in the cathedral at Geneva was a magnificent sculptured work protected by painted panels. It was dedicated to Saint Peter, patron saint of the cathedral. The town in the background of this panel is Geneva. Mont Blanc can be seen in the distance. Apart from the unusually faithful reproduction of an actual landscape, transpositions of time and place (such as this placement of a biblical scene in a medieval setting) are characteristic of Gothic painting. There is a strong Flemish influence in much of Witz's work.

ENGRAVING AND OBJETS D'ART

At the end of the 14th century and during the 15th century, the technique of printing was developed in northern Europe. It became possible to mass-produce images and texts. The printing process spread learning and knowledge across Europe and it allowed for the mass production of pictures by **engraving.**

Initially, wood engraving was used to produce playing cards and small prints. It was also used to illustrate popular texts. Engravings were usually colored by hand and included stylistic lettering known as **calligraphy.**

By the 15th century, engraving was being done on copper sheets. This development parallels the invention of movable type and the printing press. Engraving on copper was a great advance because it allowed a more exact reproduction of the original drawing and much finer detail than did wood engraving. The era of artistic engraving had begun. Martin Schongauer was one of the 15th-century engravers who represented the height of Gothic engraving. Gothic painters were inspired by Schongauer's engravings or used them as models. This type of influence was one of the first results of the mass production of images.

ANONYMOUS. *The Tree of Jesse*. Late 12th Century. Chartres Cathedral, Chartres, France.
The stained glass windows of Chartres Cathedral are among the most extensive and best preserved windows of the Gothic period. The image of the Virgin—to whom the cathedral is dedicated—occupies the central window of the

Stained Glass

During the 13th century, stained glass windows ceased to be seen merely as decoration for Gothic churches. These windows were thought of as clear walls and became an integral part of the architecture and the space within buildings.

Basically, a stained glass window consists of many multicolored pieces of glass arranged to form a figure or a scene. The pieces are held in place with strips of lead (called leading). The stained glass window would be designed by an artist, perhaps a famous painter. The glass would be arranged over the design, and colors would be chosen. Different thicknesses of glass created variations in shading and tone.

The main outlines of the design were defined by the leading. The details were painted in with vivid colors using the technique of grisaille.

The spaces assigned for windows in Gothic churches were usually tall and narrow. The themes of the artwork tended to be governed by the shape of the window frames. Sometimes the scenes were arranged in a series of **medallions**, or panels. Scenes from the Old and New Testaments were frequently used in the windows. As windows became larger, they tended to be divided horizontally.

The most spectacular of all Gothic stained glass windows are the magnificent rose windows—circular windows filled with tracery—of the Gothic cathedrals. Their messages were varied though always symbolic. Very often, the Last Judgment would be used for the windows of the western facade of a cathedral, with Christ and Mary in the windows of the north and south transepts. Among the finest of Gothic rose

presbytery. The tree of Jesse is frequently used in Gothic art. It is a symbolic representation of the lineage of Christ. The vertical orientation of this image and the imitation of a tree's foliage is well suited to the shape of the windows.

Sainte Chapelle. 1248. Paris, France.
This chapel represents the ultimate achievement in the substitution of glass for stonework in the walls of a building. This was made possible by the development of architectural techniques during the Gothic period, such as flying buttresses, that allowed the interior space of a building to be completely uncluttered. The emperor of Constantinople ordered the building of the Sainte Chapelle to house the crown of thorns and other relics. The building actually consists of two chapels, one above the other. The walls of the upper chapel have been almost completely transformed into stained glass windows that depict scenes related to the Passion of Christ.

windows are those of Notre Dame in Paris, and of eims, Chartres, Lausanne, Orvieto, and Siena.

old, Silver, and Enamel Work

In an age so devoted to refinement and luxury, the working of precious metals occupied an important place. From the beginning of the 3th century, the use of gold and silver increased—nd not just in religious works. Though few noneligious works have survived from this period, ve have records of them. The inventories of nedieval kings and queens frequently mention he names of specific jewels. The "Castle of Love" vas owned by Pedro the Ceremonious, and the Golden Foal"—one of the loveliest medieval jewels till in existence—is in the church of Altötting, ear Munich.

PERE BERNEÇ and others. Altarpiece. 14th century. Gerona Cathedral, Gerona, Spain.
This silver altarpiece, which stands on the high altar of Gerona Cathedral, was made in several stages during the middle of the 14th century. One of the most important craftsmen was Pere Berneç, who signed the base of the central scene. The piece is remarkable for the transparent enamels used to beautify the work. This altarpiece also has a canopy, or covering. It is a particularly fine example of Gothic altar decoration.

There are also crowns, scepters, and other roya pieces. Jewels for individual adornment appeare later. Drinking vessels, plates, and tableware wer luxurious works of precious metal.

No less luxurious were the pieces made fo church use. Many of those pieces have survived allowing us to study Gothic techniques o metalworking and enameling. Both those skill are closely tied to that of monumental sculpture Just as the illumination of manuscripts tended t become stylized during the Middle Ages, so to did the decorative work of goldsmiths.

The most striking technical innovation of th Gothic goldsmiths and silversmiths was th application of transparent or translucent enamel over gold or silver that had been worked in **bas relief**. This resulted in beautiful colored effects.

The main centers of production for these piece were the principal courts of Europe. Ruler commissioned the most sumptuous works an employed the finest craftspeople to create them

In the 13th century, the cult of **relics** becam

ncreasingly popular. This popularity was due to the appearance of many relics directly linked to Christ. The Sainte Chapelle in Paris was built to house the crown of thorns, a fragment of the true cross, and other precious relics.

Some of the reliquaries (containers for the

ANONYMOUS. *Virgin*. Reliquary of Jeanne d'Evreux. Pre-1339. The Louvre, Paris, France. Queen Jeanne d'Evreux gave this reliquary to the Abbey of Saint-Denis in 1339. It contained relics associated with the Virgin and is typical of the work of goldsmiths of the Gothic age. Manuscript illumination and precious metalwork are often incorrectly referred to as "minor arts." In fact, both skills were at the forefront of experimentation in form and style during the Gothic era. This piece is typically Gothic. The base is adorned with transparent enamels.

sacred relics) had the form of arks, chapels, and religious buildings. Other Gothic reliquaries were shaped like the relics they contained. Some had very fine bas-relief ornamentation.

Goldsmiths of the time demonstrated their increasing skills by making chalices, processional crosses, and other liturgical items. Some of these pieces are truly spectacular.

Tapestries

The art of tapestry flourished in Europe during the 14th century. There had doubtless been earlier experiments with tapestry, but no examples have survived.

Tapestries were produced from drawn or painted designs and were used to decorate rooms in palaces and large mansions. They also kept out some of the drafts in these buildings. The themes depicted were nearly always related to life at court or to the activities of knights. Occasionally, religious themes, chiefly from the Old Testament, were used.

Tapestries were usually designed for use in one palace, or even in one room. A complete cycle of story would be illustrated by a series of tapestries.

Making a tapestry was a long, complex task. In addition, costly materials—silks and gold thread—were needed. This limited the enjoyment of tapestries to a very wealthy few who could afford to commission them. As would be expected, production was centered where the textile industry was already developed in Europe, chiefly in the Low Countries. In Italy, other textile arts, such as embroidery, damask work, and needlework with silks, had developed and enjoyed extraordinary success.

Paris was also an important center for tapestry. The workshops at Arras in northern France

ANONYMOUS. *Vision.* Tapestry from the series *The Lady and the Unicorn.* Late 15th century. Cluny Museum, Paris, France. *The Lady and the Unicorn* is one of the most beautiful Gothic tapestry series. There are six scenes, all depicting the lady, the lion bearing a standard or banner, and the unicorn. This scenes may represent the human senses—this one possibly refers to the sense of sight, because of the mirror the lady holds. The background of vivid red is covered with floral decoration and animals. It is not known for certain where this tapestry was woven. The excellent design and refined elegance make this tapestry typical of work done during the later part of the Middle Ages.

acquired great renown and became the main producers of tapestries during the Gothic period. In England, the word "arras" was used to describe this style of wall hanging. The designs of Arras tapestry lack perspective. They usually show a large number of figures against an architectural or rural background.

Ceramics

The principal centers for the production of ceramics during the Gothic period were in Spain, where the influence of the Islamic world was felt. Ceramic production methods were Islamic, and so was the majority of the work force.

Glazing techniques using tin oxide and lead originated in the East. These were adopted in Spain and spread across Europe. These glazes produced metallic reflections and were often combined with a brilliant cobalt blue. Although ceramic designs later became more Westernized, they were never totally free from Eastern influence, nor did they develop much of a range of colors.

ANONYMOUS. Ceramic plate from Manises. 15th century. Instituto Valencia de Don Juan, Madrid, Spain.
Ceramic designs from Manises typically combined blue and another color glaze. Themes were usually limited to heraldry, inscriptions, and animals shown in hunting settings. This plate has a shield at the center, with a design resembling ivy leaves on the rest of the surface. This design was repeated fairly often throughout the 15th century. In some cases, the undersides of these plates were also decorated with patterns of animals.

Ceramics from Manises in Spain looked elegant and costly. This ensured the ceramic work a place in royal and princely palaces across Europe. Manises ceramics appear often in paintings of the time.

Ceramic pieces in more general use were often designed in shades of green and brown. Designs were inspired by the Islamic world and featured geometric patterns, animals, and persons placed face-to-face.

Ivories

Delicate ivory carving was brought to a fine degree of perfection during the Gothic period. Just when earlier uses for ivory,

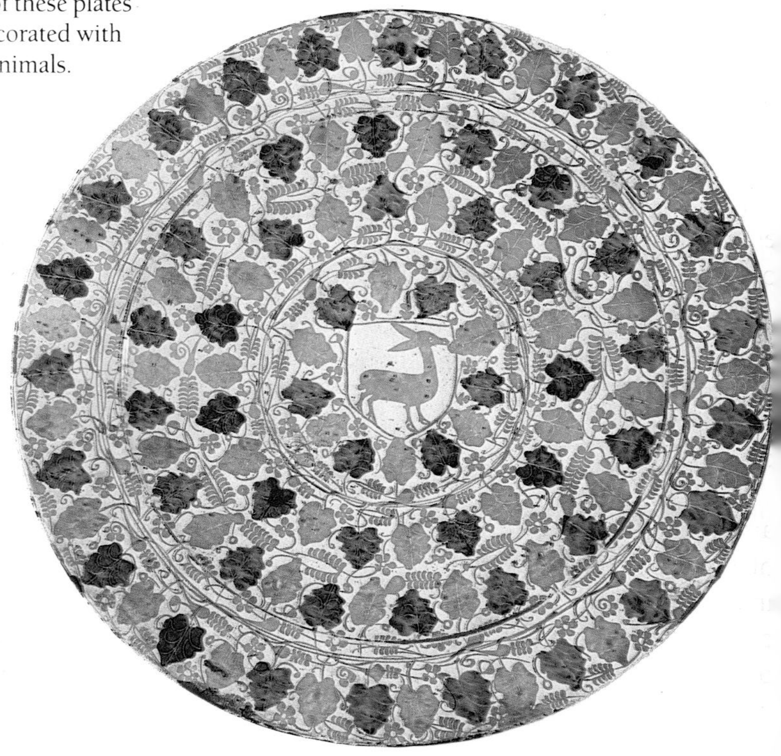

uch as decoration for book covers, seemed to be ying out, aristocratic and middle-class commis-ions for ivory objects increased. Though ivory arving is often linked to religious arts, ivory bjects are not found only in cathedrals and nonasteries. Many ivory objects were created or private use.

ANONYMOUS. Mirror cover. c. 1300. The Louvre, Paris, France.
When not being used for religious items, ivory was frequently used for small trinket boxes, chests, and mirrors. Designs reflected different aspects of court life and were frequently inspired by scenes in litera-ture, such as conversations between lovers or lovers kissing. A game of chess between lovers, shown here, was another common scene. Note the smoothness of the relief carving in this mirror cover and the supple, stylized, curvature of the figures.

Ivory carving was the work of specialists, often stablished sculptors. Of these, the most outstanding carver was Giovanni Pisano.

The main center for ivory carving was Paris, lthough there are some noteworthy examples rom English and Italian workshops. In Spain original work in ivory was limited to a few figures of Mary.

Notable ivory objects with religious themes re **diptychs** and **triptychs** carved with scenes of the Passion or the life of the Virgin. Small mages of the Crucifixion and the Virgin were also arved. The carvings often recall the sculptures of the time.

GLOSSARY

altarpiece A painted or carved work of art placed behind and above the altar of a church

ambulatory A covered walkway; the semicircular passage around the apse of a church

arch A curved structure used to span an opening such as a window or door

apse A semicircular space at the east end of the nave of a church

bas-relief Sculptural relief in which the projection from the surrounding surface is light and no part of the modeled form is undercut

buttress A projecting support built against an external wall of a building, usually to help support a vault or arch

calligraphy Decorative or formal writing executed with a quill or reed pen, or a brush

cathedral A bishop's official throne

choir An area in a church reserved for the clergy and the singing choir, usually marked off by steps, a railing, or a screen

clerestory A row of windows in the upper part of a wall, used to provide direct lighting in a church

cloister An open court attached to a church or monastery used for study, meditation, and exercise

diptych A pair of ivory carvings or panel paintings, usually hinged together

donjon The innermost and strongest structure or central tower of a medieval castle

engraving The process of incising lines into a surface to create an image

facade The principal face or front of a building

flying buttress An arched bridge above the aisles of a church that reaches from the upper nave wall out to a solid pier

gable A triangular structure above the doorway of a Gothic church

gallery The second story of a church

grisaille Painting with tones of a single color in order to give the effect of sculpture

keystone The topmost block of an arch that locks the other pieces into place

jambs The vertical sides of an opening such as a door or window

lintel A horizontal bar across the top of a window or door

medallion A panel in a wall or window bearing a sculpture or portrait

miniature A single illustration in an illuminated manuscript; a very small painting on ivory, glass, or metal

nave The central aisle of a church extending from the entrance to the apse

openwork Work that is pierced or perforated with patterns and designs

panel A wooden surface used for painting. Often two or more panels are joined together to create an altarpiece.

perspective A technique for representing spatial relationships and three-dimensional objects on a flat surface

nnacle A small, decorative structure capping a tower

olyptych An altarpiece made of several panels joined together, often hinged

ortico A covered walkway, often at the entrance of a building

resbytery The part of a church reserved for the clergy

lic An object associated with a saint or martyr

lief Carved or modeled sculpture that projects from a flat background surface

od screen A screen, frequently ornamented with sculpture, that separates the choir of a church from the nave or transept

ire A tapering structure surmounting a tower; a steeple

acery Ornamental stone ribbing and pattern work

ansept A section of a church placed at a right angle to the nave

iforium The third level of a church

iptych An altarpiece with one central panel and two hinged wings

rret A small tower

mpanum An arched area over the lintel of a door or window, frequently carved with relief sculpture

ault An arched roof or ceiling

ART THROUGHOUT THE AGES

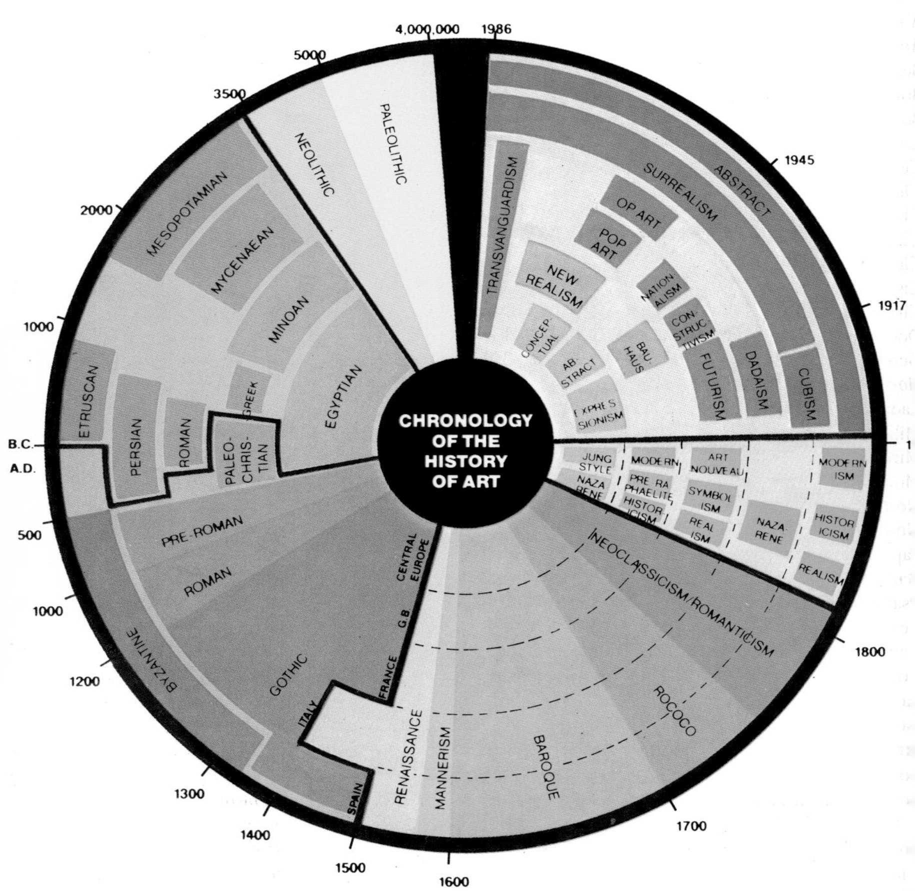

This chart shows the evolution of Western and Near Eastern art through the ages. The terms are those that art historians traditionally use to label periods of time in various cultures where definite stylistic tendencies have occurred. The books in the Key to Art series examine the interplay of artists, ideas, methods, and cultural influences that have affected the evolution of specific art styles.

INDEX OF ILLUSTRATIONS

CONTENTS

ACKNOWLEDGMENTS
A.P.: pp. 3, 23; Scala: pp. 5, 6, 8, 9, 13, 15, 26, 31, 33, 34, 38, 39, 42, 43, 44, 52-53, 54-55, 60, 69; Aisa: pp. 7, 16, 32, 37, 55, 63; Giraudon: pp. 10, 29, 40, 47, 51, 58, 59, 68; Louvre, Paris: pp. 11, 41, 45, 57, 71, 75; National Gallery, London: pp. 14, 61; Ancient Art & Architecture Collections: pp. 18, 21; Index: pp. 30, 70; Oronoz: pp. 36, 46, 48, 65, 74; Museum of Catalan Art, Barcelona: pp. 50, 64; Narodny Gallery, Prague: p. 56; Prado Museum, Madrid: pp. 62, 66; Museum of Art and History, Geneva: p. 66; Organization of National Museums: p. 73.